C E L E B R A T I O N   A N D

E X P E R I E N C E   I N

P R E A C H I N G

Celebration
and
Experience
in Preaching

HENRY H. MITCHELL

ABINGDON PRESS

Nashville

CELEBRATION AND EXPERIENCE IN PREACHING

Copyright © 1990 by Abingdon Press

This book is printed on recycled, acid-free paper.

Library of Congress Cataloging-in-Publication Data

MITCHELL, HENRY H., 1919–
    Celebration and experience in preaching / Henry H. Mitchell.
        p.   cm.
    Includes bibliographical references.
    ISBN 0-687-04744-7 (alk. paper)
    1. Preaching. I. Title.
    BV4211.2.M54   1990   90-35024
    251—dc20   CIP

ISBN 978-0-687-04744-4

Scripture quotations are from the Authorized or King James Version
of the Bible, or are the author's translation or paraphrase.

Portions of the first four chapters are either verbatim or edited
versions of Parts I and II of "On Preaching to the Whole Person,"
which appeared in the January/February and March/April editions of
the *Pulpit Digest* of 1988, vols. LXVIX, no. 489, and LXVX, no. 490.

07 08 09 10 11 12 13 14 — 27 26 25 24 23 22 21 20

Dedicated to our children:

Muriel M. Mitchell
Elizabeth Mitchell Clement
Kenneth R. Mitchell

CONTENTS

FOREWORD

What Henry Mitchell writes about preaching has been tested on the road for more than half a century and refined in the classroom for half that time. The wisdom and insights he shares have been exposed to loving critique by scores of his students, ministerial colleagues, and teachers of preaching. In addition to his professorial responsibilities, he has been at the center of an informal dialogue on preaching with friends and acquaintances from a wide cross-section of denominations and regions of the country.

I have enjoyed membership in both the formal and the informal sections of Mitchell's academy of homiletics. His *Black Preaching* (Harper & Row, 1979) helped me to affirm with pride gifts I had inherited from a vibrant African American homiletical tradition. His mentoring in the Martin Luther King, Jr., Black Church Studies Program at Colgate Rochester Divinity School deepened my understanding of the unique contribution Black preaching could make for the empowerment of the broader ministry of the Word.

As a professor of homiletics in a predominantly White seminary, I found that Mitchell's *Recovery of Preaching* provided an invaluable enrichment of perspective, when used with the bibliography of the guild. His work has a way of identifying issues largely neglected by others in the field, or at least of making much clearer those issues they often fail to emphasize.

Drawing upon his earlier volumes, Mitchell picks up the themes of celebration and "movements in consciousness," and expands upon the why and the how of these elements in the preaching task. He gives specific instructions on how to move from lackluster communication to superlative proclamation, which gets the hearers "on board" in the dynamic of the biblical story. He shows how a commitment to engaging the whole person—spirit, intuitive mind, and emotive consciousness—increases the prospect that the preaching event will be a transformative experience.

Whereas Mitchell's earlier works emphasized the Black church tradition almost exclusively as his primary source, this book acknowledges that the evangelical preaching tradition, shared by Blacks as well as Whites, has drawn from various streams to perfect a broad preaching profile. Thus one will experience this effort as a bridge across the ethnic abyss, bringing fresh strength to all who engage in the exchange. This work will break open new possibilities for those who have viewed preaching for so long as primarily a rationalistic enterprise. At the same time it will share with the opposite group a set of terms and disciplines with which to refine and focus the marvelous powers of a folk tradition.

Finally, let's give Henry Mitchell, the dean of imaging and the hearers' identification, his due. We are the recipients of his more than fifty years' labor of love to tell us what the great preachers of time all along have been saying by way of their sermons: "The people" need a picture from God to take with them on their journey; "the people" need to hear from your mouth that you have translated with your head the issues that flow through the hearts of humanity. Without minimizing the crucial significance of the cognitive dimension, Mitchell effectively questions the adequacy of theories and practices of proclamation that bow down at the altar of the enlightenment, passing over the Puritan piety of heartfelt religion. Mitchell not only calls for a proper balance of head, heart, and hands; he shows us how to do it. The cure for the "common coldness" that attends too much preaching has been made available in our lifetime. Our thanks be to God the giver and to Henry Mitchell the distributor. I expect many preachers to discover in the pages that follow the clue to a quality of delivery that will turn the experience into a very powerful occasion of celebration.

James A. Forbes, Jr.
Pastor, Riverside Church,
New York City
March 9, 1990

P R E F A C E

A N D

A C K N O W L E D G M E N T S

What is offered here in my third work on preaching is a long-simmering synthesis of two major strains of development: the "mainstream" Protestant pulpit tradition in America, and the African American church pulpit tradition. They have influenced each other ever since the First Great Awakening, but this is to bring it out in the open and provide intentionality and some detail to what has been largely a spontaneous symbiosis. Indeed, it might be fair to say that this combination of emphases on flow-in-consciousness, emotive expression, and concluding celebration represents the latest stage in the process. From here on it might be hoped that the cross-fertilization would be expedited by much more formal dialogue and publication.

On the one hand this work represents my latest progress in the analyzing and recording the best of an African American folk-pulpit tradition nearly as old as the Colonies. It was brought out of clandestine religious gatherings and shaped for the powerful propagation of the Christian faith during the First and Second Great Awakenings. It flourished underground in the South for decades prior to the Civil War. It was always intentionally experience-centered, and geared to establishing a flow in consciousness. But it was never technically described in these terms. Everybody knew that the Word had to come alive in the hearer, and there was a communal-cultural intuition about how it was to be done. But this intuition was passed on by limited oral tradition and copious example.

Then, in the last decade or so, comes a great new wave of interest in preaching among the chief American Protestant denominations. Much of what they propose, in terms like *formation* and *flow in consciousness, narrative theology* and *theological plots* and *drama,* represents real breakthroughs in homiletic theory. At least three important results have followed.

First, the supply of a terminology applicable to both cultures has made possible a new breadth of discussion across traditional lines. This discussion facilitates cross-fertilization, which enriches both traditions beyond any of our fondest expectations. The problem becomes one of providing the nuts and bolts of the potential synthesis which glows so bright in theory. This is what is attempted in this book, but not without a prior step, which is the second result.

Inside African American culture a new ferment is growing, not only for intercultural dialogue, but also for self-understanding within the culture. The tradition has to be recorded, analyzed, and reflected on before it can be shared, and this is possible in a more practical way with the emergence of a set of terms. This book includes the first application of these terms to the analysis of African American homiletic tradition. It is my hope that future works will continue the task. Another item on my hope list is a greater awareness of how the most recent theories, at least to some extent, have been road-tested for centuries in the pulpits of African American churches.

The report of these findings has already been tentatively shared in the first two issues of *Pulpit Digest* in 1988. A dialogue was instituted then which has been most helpful. It is hoped also that this will continue, and thanks are here expressed to all who have participated. Thanks are also most warmly expressed to students of the seven seminaries where I have taught or am still teaching from this work. And thanks are due the participants in seminars and workshops, colloquia and conferences on preaching across the nation. They have (with my wife and teaching partner, Ella) road-tested three earlier editions of this manuscript.

A third result, emerging from the two already mentioned, is a fresh and exciting awareness of the importance of celebration across all cultural and theological lines. We in African American tradition have cultural roots which demand that a sermon end in a celebration. For this we had a number of our own terms, such as "coming on up at the end," "the gravy," "the rousements," "the whoop," or just the generic "climax." We knew celebration to be so essential that no sermon in most quarters dared end without one. We sensed a certain artistic appropriateness and validity about celebration. But it has been only in these recent years of embryonic interchange that the deeper functions, disciplines, and effectiveness of celebration have risen, as it were, to the surface and been discussed. Celebration is probably the most significant contribution to be offered by African American tradition, and certainly it is the most important concern of this book. I dare to dream that this fresh insight into the rationale and technique for celebration will be used of God for the conservation of a useful heritage *and* the revival of the power of the preached Word among all God's children.

There is one important frustration about which the reader should know, however. It is the inability of print to signal the complete communication intended. Close associates and students constantly remind me that what is on the page doesn't really suggest its power until rendered orally. They have missed much until the same material is *heard* in a lecture. May I suggest, in my inescapable absence, that you turn up the volume a bit and first listen in your mind to what is said on the paper, or even read the sermons out loud.

When I first wrote *Black Preaching* more than twenty years ago, I forecast a day when the treasures of the ''Black'' pulpit tradition would be shared with all the world. Little did I dream that that day would already be here in 1990, and that the benefits to all concerned would be so great. It is above all that I would have asked or thought in 1965. And to God be the praise!

PART I

CONCERNING HOLISTIC PREACHING

CHAPTER 1

ON PREACHING TO THE WHOLE PERSON

And thou shalt love the Lord thy God with all thy heart, and with all thy soul, and with all thy mind, and with all thy strength: this is the first commandment.

(Mark 12:30; cf. Matt. 22:37 and Luke 10:27)

Jesus' words above, about loving God, summarize the First Commandment. They give unquestionable evidence of a deep concern in Hebrew tradition for the *holistic* commitment of persons to and in the faith. Such a commitment was seen as the very will of God. Detached, "objective" reasoning as "faith" was unthinkable to the Hebrew mindset. The word here translated "mind" is from a vocabulary that never really differentiated functions within personality. This cultural frame of reference recognized nothing short of the whole human at all times. Even without stipulating heart and soul and strength, the word *mind (dianoia)* in the text would have included understanding, feeling, and desiring—most of the conceivable facets or functions of human psyches. Yet, despite this clarity of biblical position, Western culture has for centuries preached primarily to the mental faculties, emphasizing the appeal to reason, to the virtual exclusion of other gifts. Today, many writers in the field of homiletics are confessing as much. No matter how much they may affirm sermon impact on the *"heart,"* however, typical preparation has yet to be targeted to the feelings in any disciplined way that is professionally recognized. In fact, there is still much to be learned about preaching that addresses the totality of human beings, in a manner consistent with Jesus' affirmative and holistic summary of the First Commandment. This is the task attempted here.

Patterns of sermon preparation in America's cultural mainstream suggest little awareness that preaching to the whole person requires holistic goals and methods. Two simple facts may help one perceive how true this is. One is the reality that primary concern is given to cogency; typical sermon outlines are devised on the basis of largely logical and cognitive criteria. The other fact is that the very creeds traditionally included in Christian liturgy were similarly designed; their original goal was to answer abstract theological questions in a manner that appealed to reason, and provided a basis for unity in empires and ecclesiastical bodies. The point is that this confession of faith was focused on issues almost completely irrelevant to existential concerns and human wholeness. Preaching to the whole person demands holistic goals and content, and methods that affect all sectors of human consciousness. These are prerequisite if one's efforts are to be used by the Holy Spirit to plant faith in the deepest and most complete sense.

THE HOLISTIC FAITH WE PREACH

The departures from tradition proposed here require at the outset a redefinition of faith itself. The faith assumed to be the goal of the preaching advocated is, like the methods, holistic. That is, the hearer is to be involved holistically in the sermon event, in order to beget or nourish a faith that involves the entire person. In the temptation experience, Jesus is recorded (Matt. 4:4) as quoting Deuteronomy 8:3: "It is written, Man shall not live by bread alone, but by every word that proceedeth out of the mouth of God." Although human beings need bread, Jesus is voicing the certain truth that ultimate existence is based on the very Word of God. The preached word, then, is literally to be lived by.

A common understanding of such a statement would probably be something like a set of rules by which one lives, but Jesus here is speaking of the very sustenance of life. Jesus would surely not deny the need for rules, but this Word is lived *by* in the sense that it is lived *on;* life depends on it. For Satan this response means that Jesus' integrity and wholeness as a person, his being itself, is based on the Word. One survives and copes and orders life by means of the very utterances of God to the people of God.

The minute one sees the preached word in these dimensions, it becomes apparent that the Word has to be heard in a manner that reconstitutes one's whole mode of being. The preacher's goal is to be used of God to move the hearers' supporting core beliefs and entire life-style closer and closer to the new person in Christ. This will include information and reasoning, of course, but the main goal is not informational; it is related to the depths of being, where trust *and* distrust reside. The faith referred to here is a "gut" faith, with or without the believer's ability to articulate accurately its profound significance.

Such faith is perhaps best manifested in the believer's comparatively calm behavior under stress. Persons who do not have such core trust suffer *holistically*, in that peptic ulcers, high blood pressure, and other conditions are sometimes the result of high levels of anxiety. The person blessed to possess holistic faith does everything in his or her power to solve a given problem. After that, this believer just assumes that God will do whatever else is needed, knowing that God understands the predicament and has the power and the providential intent to squeeze a good end out of it all. (*Anxiety* is another word for the inability to trust—the gut level fear that God is *not* dependable.) Healthy trust does not have to be called up by efforts initiated in the midst of the storm; it is already there, in core belief. This trust has been nurtured from holistic encounters with the Word, and it resides in the very viscera of the believer, so to speak.

A trust such as this becomes the foundation for all other aspects of the Christian's life and work. One can seek first the kingdom of God with much greater ease, when one trusts God so fully. The value system of the Sermon on the Mount is not feared as a great invitation to undue risk. Likewise, the call of Christ to the costly, prophetic reshaping of human institutions is more gladly undertaken in trust, and more effectively accomplished by a person at peace. In other words, the priestly effort to propagate a holistic faith is not to be mistaken for individualistic escapism or social irresponsibility. It is actual empowerment for the greatest challenges the Kingdom has to offer a seriously practicing Christian. Indeed, the call of God to service can best be heard and obeyed by in-depth believers. Others must struggle much harder to avoid healthfully the pitfalls of surface conformity and willingly and trustingly obey God from the heart.

A GROWING REORIENTATION

This brings to mind a glaring oversight many of us have "discovered" only recently: Such a faith as this is not begotten by human reasoning, nor does it reside in the cognitive regions of the brain. Modern researchers are saying that it resides in the intuitive region, that great, right-brain storehouse, whose content has not been entered into the human data bank by rational criteria and processes. One must add that faith also resides in the emotions. If fear is an emotion, then so is its opposite, trust. In other words, if one's faith has no emotive dimension and involvement, it is cold and without depth. But more of this later. The point to be emphasized here is that sane faith must be born *in* a reasonable encounter, but it is not born *of* rational argument. Nor does it reside primarily in the spheres of the mind where logic is the dominant function.

This I should have learned during my teen years. It was then, as I first grappled with intellectual questions, that I was exposed to the apostle Paul's parallel insight (originally offered, of course, in a context of encouragement to endurers of suffering): "For we are saved by hope: but hope that is *seen* is not hope: for what a man seeth, why doth he yet hope for?" (Rom. 8:24, emphasis added). The power to verify things rationally is a form of *"sight,"* which automatically removes the matter from the realm of faith.

David Roberts at Union Theological Seminary told us the same thing in a philosophy of religion class. He equipped us to defend ourselves against logical positivists and other devotees of scientific verifiability—the idolatry which insists that *all* truth can be measured and proved in a lab. He advised, "Just ask them how they *know* the assumptions underlying *their* system of thought. Don't accept the defensive role; put *them* on the defensive. You see, their basic position is one of faith and not sight, just like yours." It worked! I have had marvelous success by taking the offensive, just as he advised. But it took many years for me to see what this appraisal of reason meant, in terms of the focus of effort in sermon preparation. If I couldn't use pure reason to argue a logical positivist into faith, then why should I expect that reason, from the pulpit or elsewhere, to beget faith in anybody else?

Come to think of it, this is a good thing. Suppose faith were a function of reason, and salvation a response to established data or truth (cf. Pannenberg below). Then the ordinary and less than ordinary IQ would be at a distinct disadvantage. To say nothing of the questions all of this would raise concerning the justice of God. Some of the choicest saints I knew in the pastorate were not supposedly well endowed with intellect. Their speech may have been assumed to betray a poverty of thought, but their lives as a whole spoke most eloquently of their true system of core beliefs. We more ordinarily gifted folk can rejoice that faith is not restricted to those who can grasp x number of propositions.

Fred Craddock puts it this way: "Long after a man's head has consented to the preacher's idea, the old images may still hang in the heart. . . . The longest trip a person takes is that from head to heart" (*Authority*, p. 78). The faith on which people bet their very lives comes *not* because one has heard and understood a great flow of logical persuasion, though the love of God demands that we understand all we can. Rather, it is the fruit of holistic encounter, with familiar images, whatever one's intelligence might be.

Nevertheless, the idea that reason as such has some sort of content, and that faith in some sense is *born* of reason (= "sight"), dies hard. No less a serious and highly respected theologian than Wolfhart Pannenberg writes that "believing trust cannot be separated from the trusting person's belief in the truth of the thing in which he trusts and towards which his trust is directed" (*Creed*, p. 6). In his laudable crusade to free the Christian faith from "subjective tastes," which have no "universally binding power," he declares the purpose of theology to be the giving of a "rational account of the truth of faith" (*Basic*, p. 53). He softens this a bit elsewhere when he says, "It is true that in order to be faith in the full sense of the word, faith does not need to be conscious of these reasons in every case and above all not in their ultimate clarity and form. It is sufficient that the decision of faith actually rests on reasons that will hold up" (*Theology*, p. 271). Many believers still consider themselves looking to reason to produce rather than to process the tenets of faith, all of which are beyond either proof or disproof. As Augustine argued, one has to believe first, in order to have knowledge. The very world view (or vision of reality) that provides the frame of reference within which we know anything at all is a priori—a matter of faith, not sight.

THE ROLE OF REASON

Lest it appear that I am completely ruling out rational concerns in the preaching event, let me quickly provide clarity about the indispensable role of human reason. Every sermon must make *sense;* it must be manifestly reasonable and generally consistent with an orderly understanding of God's creation and our experience in it. Otherwise the subsection of the rational mind or ego that *monitors* such things will shut down one's receptivity to the message. Monitoring is a vital function, and without it people are not only vulnerable; they are no longer sane. However, although reason clears the way or opens the gate to the intuitive, it does *not* itself *beget faith*. Therefore, when one has arrived at an acceptably cogent flow chart or outline of sermon ideas, one has only begun the preparation by ensuring that its very flow will not be an intellectual obstacle. The demanding task of giving birth to faith and nourishing it remains. One has yet to address the more operatively relevant realms of human personality, such as intuition and emotion (of which much more will be said later), where faith is generated and retained.

Thus, close to this function of the rational processes as monitor is the responsibility for clearing away intellectual obstacles to faith. The book of Hebrews quite soundly declares that people seeking God must *first believe* that God exists (11:6). For a thinking Christian to arrive at this starting place of true core belief demands initially that honest questions be given adequate answers. One dare not open the door of deep consciousness to this nonrational process of faith until one has either a good answer to vital questions, or a sound awareness that this is the type of question to be answered not in time but in eternity. It is never healthful to by-pass this questioning function arbitrarily. "Only believe!" cannot be sound advice unless these obstacles have been dealt with. Those who love God with all their minds express that love by seeking reasonable answers to genuine questions, wherever possible, instead of overworking the essential blindness of faith.

On the other hand, people can think they know more and need less than they actually do. For instance, the illusion of autonomous reason needs to be cleared away. This is the frame of reference that includes the idea that intelligence can begin as a blank slate and generate its own content. Appropriate use of reason makes us face our unyielding limits, thus opening the way to faith.

Reason has many other functions to perform in connection with faith; it is never absent. The very formulation of faith into an utterance capable of being communicated and understood requires language as a tool of *rational* expression. Belief becomes rationally expressed the minute it is shared with any other person. Indeed, even personal reflection requires this same component of expression. Faith is not reason, but it can never be shared, talked of, or even thought about without a reasonable sequence of words and flow of images.

Then there is the whole function of keeping one's faith *coherent*, free of self-contradiction. This suggests the orderly reflection about God, labeled *theology*. But it is not for "theologians" only; it is a necessity for all believers. Peter (who needed Silas to do his writing for him) urged all Christians to be able to give a reasonable or coherent report of their hope (I Pet. 3:15) to anyone who might ask. One cannot argue folks into belief, but all witnesses bear the obligation to establish the internal coherence and intellectual integrity of the testifier. This includes the rational cogency of the system of core beliefs and the style of life that the witnesses have built upon their unprovable and all-important assumptions of faith.

Two other functions of reason come to mind in connection with belief. One is that of motivator in the listening process. Every sermon needs a carefully chosen introduction, designed to raise compelling questions and whet the hearer's curiosity or appetite for truth. Narratives and related genres also create a *suspense* that causes hearers to maintain attention and take careful note of all that is recounted. This suspense is essentially rational, but it impels one to remain involved and enter holistically into the deeper realms of meaningful vicarious experience. Intellectual curiosity both leads to the fountain and helps the hearer to drink experientially.

The other function of reason has to do with the *application* of faith to the life of the hearer and to all of life. Sermons are expected to help hearers apply the affirmations of their faith to needs in the real world. The book of James suggests that faith without works is dead (2:20). Except for the extreme rarity of a miracle, working faith is irrevocably committed to the logic of the workaday world. Works born of the deepest trust still have to be planned and executed quite rationally for the most part, and sermons have to be written with this in mind.

These six functions of reason are vitally important. They apply before, during, and after a faith-begetting experience in which the heart is strangely warmed, or the soul meets Christ on a basis beyond but not contradictory of reason. It is time now to turn to how faith is begotten.

THE BEGETTING OF FAITH: INTUITIVE CONSCIOUSNESS

No amount of isolated or pure reason can cause belief to happen. Reason may make straight the highway or prepare the path, but faith invades our lives through the *intuitive* and *emotive* sectors of consciousness. How, then, does one affect the intuitive and emotive regions of human personality, given the six indispensably supportive functions of rationality? The intuitive realm is affected more directly by *experiential* encounter.

The "tapes" of intuition contain impressions gathered and stored during the flow of life. This input is not examined, adopted, or organized in a *consciously* rational manner. It includes a wide variety of insights from culture, family, church, school and community, and individual experience. The intuitive realm includes such things as taste for foods, responses to varieties of people, and the way one views the world—one's belief system. Intuition can be guilty of harboring prejudice, but it may also contain most if not all of our highest and most valid values and insights. Indeed, its wisdom is quite frequently superior to that of rational consciousness.

In *Intuition and Ego States,* psychiatrist Eric Berne reported on intuited predictions of the responses of inductees, made during the essentially intuitive examinations (of 40 to 90 seconds) for World War II. They were surprisingly accurate. Other tests of accuracy showed a rate of 55 percent on speedy hunches, and 14 percent when the certified professionals had the time to be deliberate (pp. 7-10). In effect, Berne was saying that psychiatrists who employed spontaneous hunches based on body signals and other subtle data were more often correct than those using complicated, consciously rational criteria. All of us, including psychiatrists, make many correct decisions intuitively. We live our lives daily from this data base or a-rational pool of wisdom. The fact that at least much of this storehouse is verifiably sound, and that all faith is in this category, argues for much greater concern among preachers about how to help persons improve these intuitive "tapes" or habitual replays of response to particular circumstances.

There is an account in Mark (9:16-29) which illustrates this understanding of intuition and how it relates to belief. When Jesus probed the faith of the demented boy's father, the father replied tearfully, "Lord, I believe; help thou mine unbelief." He was implying that if he had not given intellectual assent to Jesus' power, he would never have brought his son there in the first place. However, he still had a knot in the pit of his stomach, and his intuitive consciousness wasn't convinced at all. He needed help in the place where the real faith is. "Help thou mine unbelief." And this is where most people need the greatest assistance. Even those who have great intellectual obstacles to faith still need this kind of ministry after they have learned how to use reason to clear away most of their questions and challenges. Rational screening certifies only that it is safe to open the door, as it were, to the room where the intuitive tapes are kept.

One's principal locus of belief *and* unbelief is inside this deep chamber of intuition, and beyond the direct reach of propositional communication, or logical argument.

It should not be surprising, then, to find that in the providence of God, this intuitive channel of communication should be used by the Spirit in the begetting and nourishment of faith. Here one can take no personal credit for processing effectively the affirmations of faith; the glory belongs to God. The varieties of intelligence quotients are not relevant, since faith cometh not by rational accomplishment. It is required only that one love God with *all* one's mind, whatever the IQ.

The question then arises regarding what means of communication can reach the intuitive consciousness of a wide spectrum of intelligence quotients at the same time. What methods are best used of God to "over-record" or replace the tapes of childhood terrors and distrust, and otherwise strengthen the tapes of trust? The answer, as already stated, is still experiential encounter, but what does this mean?

The term *experiential encounter* is used here to denote a homiletical plan in which the aim is to offer direct or vicarious encounters with and experiences of truths already fully certified as biblical, coherent, and relevant. Sermons are reasonable and relevant sequences of biblical affirmations planted in or offered to the intuitive consciousness of hearers, by way of what might be called homiletical coworkers with the Spirit. This work is done by means of an assortment of rhetorical vehicles, or literary genres, which stimulate the hearer to identify with and take part in these very meaningful experiences. One is helped personally or vicariously to enter the spiritual-theological dynamics of an *encounter* with the Godhead, or a fellowship with biblical or other historical or current characters, and the miracle of faith takes place. The fact that we can attempt to describe it all by using such terms as *tapes* does not diminish the miracle one whit. We preachers simply have a better idea of how to talk about where we think God is working, and how. (By all means, let us avoid the erroneous impression that this is in any way related to behaviorist psychology.) These insights only make the sermons more useful and the preacher a better instrument in the hand of God. The intuitive impact of experiential encounter is a very important part of the resources by which God moves to create the miracle of faith.

Another resource used of God is emotive consciousness, which will be addressed in the section following. This sector of consciousness also can be greatly affected by rhetorical vehicles and literary genres, and emotive expression can make them even more effective. Fred Craddock says that "the presence of a full set of emotions is no evidence of the absence of intelligence . . . . Effective preaching reflects the minister's open receptivity to those life scenes which are noticeably emotional in flavor but which constitute memorable and important stations along the way most people travel" (*Authority,* p. 85). We will turn in chapter 2 to the genres reaching both the emotive and intuitive.

THE BEGETTING OF FAITH: EMOTIVE CONSCIOUSNESS

There exists a widespread, often unconscious, and rigid opposition to rejoicing in the presence of God, as an act of true adoration. The conscious and unconscious restraints of the preacher-liturgist are contagious. Thus the pastor dare not complain that the congregation simply does not loosen up, when in fact the main source of inhibition in worship may well be in the pulpit. We need, then, to develop an understanding of these restraints before we can devise a strategy for breaking them down—to generate what might be called an analytical rationale for this *un*-analytical phenomenon called emotion in worship. This is especially necessary in the light of the significance here placed on sermonic celebration.

The apostle Paul implied that three of the greatest goals in life were faith, hope, and love (I Cor. 13:13), each of them heavily involving *emotions.* This gives preaching a set of goals which inescapably includes those questionable human feelings so long and seriously shied away from. To avoid them is to miss the most important and powerful aspects of human personality.

Expressive or emotional celebration should be understood as *thoroughly biblical.* The Deuteronomic admonition is one in many: "And ye shall rejoice before the Lord your God" (12:12). Many of the most significant and moving passages in the Bible are characterized by praise and celebration. Few Christians are probably aware of just how *un*biblical it is to be as solemn and stern as most worshipers in Western culture tend to be.

The traditional use of the word *Celebration* in connection with the mass of the Roman Catholic church is indicative of a historical association of worship with emotional rejoicing. Again, the Shorter Catechism of the Presbyterian churches plainly states that the chief end of humankind is to glorify and *enjoy* God forever. Yet the worship of virtually every mainline denomination is severely inhibited emotionally. Even now, as these words are read, there likely are residues of sincere resistance to any serious practice of authentic, emotional celebration.

I do not speak as an outsider, because I have often reacted according to very Western expectations. Some years ago I visited an Ethiopian Orthodox church in Addis Ababa. There I saw "debtura" (somewhere between deacons and clergy) dancing with great dignity beside the sanctuary. Their flowing robes and huge drum made an impressive spectacle, but my first impulse was to view it as a bit silly. It took a little time for me to become sensitive to the fact that this type of worship was in a category to which *all* Christians should relate easily. In fact, in the debtura's efforts to follow David and the Bible literally, the real complaint could have been that they were actually too *discreet*.

It disturbed me that I, a product of African American culture, should be inhibited about joining with those debtura. I enthusiastically affirm authentic shouting; I fully consider it a blessing. But though I accept and rejoice in this much more dramatic form of celebration, the idea of those dignified, robed elders dancing before God, found in my unconscious depths some irrational resistance. This despite the fact that dancing is so important in African American culture, and that it is so acceptable in theory.

The experience of this one person illustrates the penetration of Western dualism among educated Americans generally. Any dancing, especially among nineteenth-century Protestants, was an activity of the "evil flesh," rather than an art form. To break out of this cultural straitjacket it is important to visualize and understand that these inhibitions are opposed to the very will of God.

A more detailed look at the cultural roots of these inhibitions may also help. Their origins are in an ancient Greek dualism of flesh and spirit. Some four centuries before Christ, a group called the Stoics became important in Greek culture. Possibly under the influence of oriental religions encountered during the movements of the troops of Alexander the Great, the Stoics launched a much needed reform against excesses common to agrarian folk religions. In order to eliminate ritual intoxication and sexually explicit fertility rites, it seemed necessary to remove all passion and deep feelings. Thus they placed emotion of all kinds under suspicion. Because of Neo-Platonism and the strong influences of scholar-theologians such as

Augustine, this dichotomy between body and spirit persisted into the Renaissance and the eighteenth-century Enlightenment. In fact, despite the contemporary hue and cry for holistic approaches affirming high emotion, most of middle-class Western society today is far better at discussing emotive celebration than at practicing it.

As a result of this history of more than two thousand years, the word *emotion* itself has suffered from gross misrepresentation. All too often the term seems to connote only the lower emotions: fear, lust, hate, prejudice, and paranoid distrust. We confuse "emotion and emotionalism, defining the quality by its extreme" (Craddock, *Authority,* p. 85). In point of fact, the word denotes the whole spectrum, high and low, good and less than good, intense as well as moderate. So the oft maligned category of emotion includes the highest goals of all preaching, and every preacher must come to affirm and be at ease expressing godly emotion.

Oddly enough, we have considered it quite acceptable for advertisers and merchants to deal in emotions in the blatant pursuit of commercial gain. Yet we preachers have been supposed to seek the salvation and maturation of precious souls under a mandate that allows only the Holy Spirit to stir the emotions, directly and unaided by any understanding or action on our part. We feel we dare not become involved in such things. Our own feelings are considered to be insufficiently holy for the house of God and the usages of worship. But there is hope; this would seem to be the sort of "demon" that, when it can be named, can be cast out.

We can't dance freely like David and the Ethiopian debtura, but knowing the nature of these undercurrents, we could become more spontaneous. It may not be easy to switch our intuitive responses and those of our audiences to freely expressive celebration. It will require very slow and purposeful effort to accomplish the change of cultural biases and expectations, but it can be done. We call such changes "acculturation."

To start this process we must understand that emotions control so much of a person's total experience that psychiatrists devote more time to emotion than to anything else. In this significant new awareness, many thoughtful people today are at least theoretically committed to the *idea* that we should no longer be ashamed of our emotions. Grown men are now advised to cry in public and cease repressing their deep feelings. Many learned clergy have even come to appreciate when they can report that after the sermon there was hardly a dry eye in the house. Of course they don't want to gain a reputation for being "tear-jerkers," like many star preachers of the media, but there is something about emotion much too essential to be ceded exclusively to the counterfeiters.

It should come as no surprise that one can find help toward the removal of inhibitions from psychiatrists and others in the healing arts. It was they who alerted us to the perils of dualism, and they have long urged a holism that would permit joyous dance and song. What they have advised about getting in touch with one's emotions is readily accomplished in the accepting, permissive environment of a worshiping family of God. That is, if and when one can slowly acculturate them to openness of mind and spirit on the matter.

Thus, to remove inhibitions, we have to become *intentional* about emotion in worship as a whole. We have always spoken against lukewarm or cold worship, even though we have not worked sufficiently hard to grasp what *warm* worship might be. Preaching, as the key element in Protestant worship, has been all along under the obligation to be warm, or emotionally moving. But we have not faced squarely the emotional character of faith and hope and love. So it is not hard to see why we haven't figured out how to communicate with and feed emotional entities. It is time to deal with the nurture of faith by means of warm and intentionally emotive sharing of the gospel, concluding with sound and spontaneous emotional expressions called "celebration."

The powerful effects of emotion must begin to be systematically utilized, rather than merely tolerated. This is mandated, if faith at the level of core belief and practice is to grow. Just as muscles must be exercised to develop physically, so must feelings. For this precise purpose worship must now be planned, as well as preparation for preaching. A congregation sings "O for a thousand tongues to sing my great Redeemer's praise," and the emotive joy of singing nurtures praise and faith in the process. They sing "It is well with my soul," and this emotionally moving affirmation strengthens their tapes of trust. It is etched, as it were, on "fleshy tablets" of the soul, which sings it wholeheartedly, through the involvement of the voice and the whole person that goes with it. The effect is neither mechanical nor final, but it has significant influence, as empowered by the Holy Spirit. Just as we have chosen moving hymns, so must we choose elements in preaching that exercise high emotions like faith-trust, love, and hope.

The celebration techniques suggested later as essential to *every* sermon are so important for just this reason; they are not mere cultural distinctives of a particular ethnic group. It is universally true that people recall far better what they have celebrated well. And they are far more apt to grow in Christian behavior-areas about which they have authentically rejoiced. One of my D.Min. students named Frank Thomas says bluntly that "they will neither remember nor practice what they have not celebrated." Emotion may be dealt with irresponsibly and unethically by some, but it must be dealt with in *some* way by *all* who would preach for the holistic growth of persons.

This is far from anti-intellectual. Educational research has confirmed the idea that what we celebrate (get emotional about) we retain far longer. Educators have joined the healers in affirming that celebration provides what I have mentioned as the "ecstatic reinforcement" of the lesson or content offered in the sermon. George Leonard, former editor of *Look* magazine, reported in his book *Education and Ecstasy* that children read best and remembered most the things about which the teachers helped them to be glad. Celebration is therefore to be sought, among many other reasons, for the way in which it can lift up the "meat" of the message and render it unforgettable. But intellectual recall is not all. There is a sense in which the depths of human intuition are closely related to the emotions, which causes the joy to affect values and levels of trust. High commitment and deep trust are far more likely to develop in an emotionally charged atmosphere. The joyous singing of the Civil Rights era, like earlier songs in labor unions and army contingents, became the very backbone of the mass movement. And many a television news report of even the recent Chinese uprisings and the movements against the Iron Curtain has shown hundreds of thousands united and empowered by emotional singing and shouted slogans. There is that much strength in commitment, which, when holistic, involves intuition and emotion, as well as logic.

Western Christianity has begun to give lip service to this holistic ideal of celebration. Biblical scholars of varying positions seem to agree that the dualism apparent in passages like Paul's lament in Romans (7:24) is not real. Paul's own more Hebraic ideas, then, were colored by the use of his family's second language and culture. The surface reading of Paul, combined with the association of emotion with the supposedly evil flesh, has had a lot to do with the inability of many to take seriously our first biblical injunction to "rejoice before the Lord." But that is changing.

The ultimate price for failing to nurture authentic celebration is that joy inhibited in expression is joy diminished or outright lost. The manners in which it is expressed may vary greatly; all "shouting" is not equally audible. But genuine joy does not exist without some form of release or expression. Blessings lifted up in praise are blessings enjoyed or celebrated on an unlimited re-run basis, to use the summer television figure. The tragic implications are either that the sermon without a celebration is without some portion of the Word worthy of such, or that the inhibition toward deserved celebration and rejoicing causes the material preached to lose its greatest possible effect within the total person.

One place to initiate the process of acculturation is in areas where we already accept celebration: poetry, music, and drama. A flat reading of a poem would be readily rejected. It must be read dramatically throughout, and it must rise to a kind of climactic utterance at the end. A cantata, like a symphony, is required to increase in intensity as it approaches the grand finale. The audience intuitively awaits the crescendo, when the theme is finally restated and lifted to its highest expression. In religious drama, the same sequence would apply, with the expectation revolving around the resolution of the conflict. Again, following the rules of art, the dramatic intensity reaches its zenith and the play draws to an exciting and satisfying conclusion. No art form is allowed simply to dribble to the end or peter out.

Whole liturgies need to be reconsidered in artistic terms, and this applies especially to the sermon. Although no one should overload the preaching role and expect it to generate miracles, it is a fact that the sermon is the facet of worship over which the minister has the greatest and most direct control. And the acceptability of celebration is more likely to be won here than anywhere else, albeit subtly and by no means in confrontation. It is not an overstatement to say that artistry will win its own acceptance in the intuitive depths of the worshiper, after the rationale has been accepted and a process of intentional emotion has been implemented with sensitivity.

A hearty minority of creative modern Christians have already taken up the challenge. Some have choreographed interpretive dance programs as acts of worship. Others seek to express themselves more freely than standard culture by using instruments such as guitars. One must applaud their commitment, yet most of those who join in the applause find it hard to worship authentically in these new and unavoidably alien modes. It takes a long time to acculturate away from deeply entrenched patterns of worship. And a wise and intentional process, involving all of any congregation, will be required to move peacefully into the growth now so obviously needed in connection with emotions and worship.

SOME WORKING UNDERSTANDINGS CONCERNING EMOTION

As one launches into what is for some a strange new world of intentional emotive expression, the excesses once assumed universal must somehow be ruled out and guaranteed against. Since there may have been no cultural expectations or other restraints in place, one needs what might be called working understandings with which to begin. In some respects it might be called a code of professional ethics. Whatever the name, one needs the security of established patterns of practice as protection against error. One also needs the respect of the constituency, which goes with the observance of an emerging canon of rules and regulations. As one born and reared in a more expressive culture than that of the American majority, I find it not difficult to propose such a set of understandings, since they have been at work in my world all my life.

Our first understanding is to practice an irrevocable commitment to high purpose, and to the use of appeals directed to the highest emotions. Evoking tears must never be an end in itself, or a means of manipulating monetary gifts, not even for supporting a world hunger project. Patronizing pity, so common earlier in the twentieth century among programs directed to the so-called heathen, is far less than truly Christian, and sinfully smug besides. Powerful emotional impact should be viewed in the same way one views dynamite. It can be most destructive when not used for the purposes for which it was made. The construction of roads and dams is impossible without dynamite. Likewise, the appeal to high emotion is required in the softening of the low emotion of stony pride, or the commitment of persons to forgiveness, or unity or hard work for world peace. Furthermore, emotional needs can be met only by means involving those same emotions. The discouragement of low emotions, the development of love and other high emotions, the commitment of the will of persons to the will of God, and the healing of hearers in need of emotional and spiritual health—all these demand that sermons have emotional impact harnessed to these high purposes.

Once this is settled, we should be freed up to be spontaneous and receive and use our full potential under the Holy Spirit. James A. Forbes offers a word of advice in this connection (*The Holy Spirit and Preaching,* p. 94): "Rather than getting bogged down over specific manifestations [of emotional expressiveness], we should focus on how we can be empowered as a result of receiving the Spirit." The greatest healings and empowerment often come with the least predictable expressions.

Second, we are obliged to avoid a message unless we feel deeply about the subject. If the preacher does not care *greatly* about the text and its meaning for the hearers, then why should they? The audience takes its subtle but powerful cues from the preacher. False or insincere facsimiles of emotion on the part of the preacher may deceive some, but they never have real spiritual depth and effect. The spoken word has power to move persons only to the extent that it has already moved the speaker.

Related to this second understanding is a third: the fact that emotion travels between the members of a warm and caring fellowship by *contagion.* This is surely not a fresh revelation to anyone who has ever attended a Christian funeral. The same is true of the touching movie in which rank strangers are moved together by a common identification with the film's characters. The hymn speaks truthfully about some of our experiences when it says that "we share our mutual woes." The power of this contagion is perhaps best validated when persons who are determined not to cry with the majority of an audience are utterly defeated. This offers sweeping challenges to the discipline of sermon preparation, and to the integrity of the preacher in the uses made of this inevitable contagion.

Reading it another way, there is a sense in which the Holy Spirit has allies in the congregation. The more outwardly spontaneous persons help those who are more subtly inhibited by both identification and contagion, within limits. This tends to free the latter to manifest more feeling, thus enhancing their own experience of the Word. This does not necessarily imply histrionic outbursts; an atmosphere may be emotionally charged with no obvious sounds or easily visible expressions. The preacher ought not to work at eliciting overt evidence of in-depth response. The spiritual-emotional quality of the preacher and the more liberated hearers will communicate without crass cues and the clamor of claques. Within the cultural expectations of any community of worshipers, the Holy Spirit is, after all, the primary "mover and shaker." Whatever the apparent dynamics, the

Holy Spirit has so fixed it that there can never be human predictions of results, nor may humans ever take credit.

Fourth, ponder the threatening fact that emotional considerations must be a part of sermon preparations from the very *outset*. Knowing that emotion is inescapable, the preacher must weigh each homiletical move for impact or effect, making sure that, so far as is in his or her power, the emotional involvement and suspense ascend progressively, to the final celebration. This concluding element is the essential ecstatic reinforcement of the Word for all people. There will be more on this subject in chapter 3, on outlines. Suffice it to say that this sort of planned timing of impact is not to be mistaken for what is pejoratively referred to as "manipulation." This is high art, as well as universal emotional logic.

Just as a dramatist writes a play whose acts move up to the resolution of the conflict, and just as a composer creates a symphony whose movements climb to the last crescendo, a sermon lifts up and finally celebrates its Good News. The logic of emotive consciousness is as important and coherent as the logic of human reason. Human emotion instinctively requires that the impact escalate, and it assumes closure when peak and downturn are signaled. All beyond this is anticlimactic, losing attention automatically. The logic of reason is not to be ignored because of this; the two logics must be synthesized, in order to provide experiential encounter for the whole person. The Holy Spirit can be counted on to use this more insightful and disciplined preparation to create and nurture new persons in Christ. This has always been the case with the most powerful preachers of all cultures and schools of theology.

Finally, the preacher needs *carefully* to select vivid details. Oft times it is the details which determine how deeply involved the hearer will be in the experiential encounter. The associations called forth may be emotionally cathartic and healing of pain; they may be feelings of righteous indignation; or they may be joyous, irrepressible waves of praise and celebration. Whatever the character of the response, deep emotions are moved to expression by identification with familiar specifics of place, problem, or other detail. The very word *identification* literally denotes emotional bonding. However much the details seem intellectually important, they gain their spiritual impact primarily from the way they move the hearer toward *feelings* of bonding with protagonists and problems and potentials, to the end of growth for the hearer toward newness in Christ.

The sermon and the worship environment encourage the hearer to express feeling in a permissive and supportive setting. The vital connection between the hearer and the movement in the sermon is a matter of feeling-with, provided that the word has passed the entrance tests of coherence. This greatly healing and liberating experience acquires ecstatic, celebrative dimensions, which reinforce the encounter. This occurs in large part because of the self-recognition and identification born of the careful selection of descriptive details.

One easily senses how this process worked in a Women's Day sermon at a church in California. The assigned biblical theme came from Luke 8:43-48, and concerned the woman with the issue of blood. Ella P. Mitchell, the preacher, told the story in carefully expanded detail. She used modern medical terms to describe the various diagnoses offered by the series of physicians to whom the woman had paid her life savings. The largely female audience identified and "came aboard," each as her own malady was mentioned. Or they related to one of the diagnoses in someone dear to them. The effect was awesome. The message of healing faith was planted deep, beyond all forgetting, by using emotional identification with this hemorrhaging woman who dared to touch the hem of Jesus' garment.

Access to emotive consciousness may be gained powerfully and unashamedly through well-timed and carefully chosen configurations of detail, both biblical and nonbiblical. This is altogether fitting and proper, since Jesus himself did it so well and often, and since it is employed in the lofty and challenging task of being used by God to generate deep emotional and spiritual growth. People need desperately to grow up unto Christ in all sectors of consciousness (Eph. 4:15), and the emotive is often the key to both retention and motivation. It is quite common to hear conversations about how psychiatry is used to heal *emotional* disorders, yet too often we preach to every sector save that one. To opt to deal with fewer than all the sectors of human consciousness is to fail willfully to deal with the whole person. To struggle to overcome cultural biases against the emotive, and to help others to do so, may well become the most rewarding enterprise of an entire career.

In the chapters that follow, the details mentioned above are employed in the various literary genres and in proper sequence, to achieve the high purpose of new creatures in Christ, growing up to him in all aspects of human personality by means of identification, encounter, and celebration.

CHAPTER 2

THE GENRES:
VEHICLES FOR ENCOUNTER

*All these things spake Jesus unto the multitude in parables; and
without a parable spake he not unto them.*
(Matt. 13:34; cf. Mark 4:33-34)

The Synoptic Gospels, Matthew, Mark, and Luke, clearly
establish that the Jewish culture of Jesus' day was strong on
communication by parable, and that our Lord was master of the art of
using them. In *The Parables of Jesus,* George Buttrick (p. xiii) agreed
with both Mark and Matthew that this style was Jesus' "characteristic
message." He went on to say that parables were Jesus' most
rememberable and persuasive method, accomplishing what a prose
homily could never do in either *retention* of ideas or movement of
hearers to *response*. In fact, neither the supposedly simple nor the
learned can properly understand Jesus without examining the richness
of the parables. They are far more powerful than abstract essays and
sermons, expressing symbolically that which escapes the narrow
bounds of literal, direct discourse. Jesus built his own preaching
ministry on parables.

It appears, then, that Western culture has strangely overlooked
Jesus' example, as well as the related fact that art is still so superior to
argument for preaching purposes. Today's audiences still remember
the *stories* best, and these also move them most. But the simplicity of
this shattering fact misleads the sophisticated theologian. Even the
recent interest in narration is given a complicated title: "narrative
theology." Perhaps it is too painful to concede the superiority of
"primitive" folk culture's encouchment of the most profound
wisdom in tales. Syllogism will never be able to match symbol in the
utterance of the unspeakable riches of the gospel, and one can start no
earlier than now to apply this wisdom to the preparation of sermons.

The superiority of tales and the like lies in the fact that people "see"
the issue more clearly in pictures and plots. Indeed, they not only

grasp ideas better; they also encounter them with their whole personhood, because they identify with the details and personalities and their activities. The truth for which the narrative is told is encountered and experienced vicariously. Thus, the idea is clarified and retained, while the encounter adds the stimulus to growth. So the "bottom line" of love, trust, commitment, and service can be taught and caught by the genres or vehicles of encounter, which in various ways function as a parable.

Here is a partial list of these vehicles of meaning:

- The Narrative
- The Character Sketch
- The Group Study
- The Dialogue
- The Monologue or Testimony
- Metaphors, Similes, and Analogs
- The Stream of Consciousness

All of these literary or folk genres are effective for reasons related to the effectiveness of Jesus' parables. In every case they amount to something placed "alongside" contemporary life, which relates to the root meaning of the word *parable*. To the old Hebrew query, "To what shall I liken this?" every one of these genres is used to provide an answer. The pervasiveness of this cry for parallel insight comes from the fact that these genres plant and water better than other types of spoken communication. They involve the hearer experientially. All preachers would be well advised in the mode of the credit card commercial: "When preaching, don't be caught without these vehicles."

Although the ideal sermon might be said to be a one-story or one-figure sermon, in which the end of the sketch or stream is the end of the sermon, most will involve more than one of these genres. Although one-story sermons may well be the art of preaching at its best, few stories from the Bible provide adequate detail for journeyman preachers to construct a tale that consumes twenty minutes. Most of us will do well to use shorter stories as mini-experiences, to illumine and render experiential the points or stages in the sermon. David Buttrick appropriately calls them "*moves*" (*Homiletic,* pp. 23-36). Straying still farther from single-narrative artistry, some preachers are quite effective at using a story simply as a frame on which to hang striking and relevant asides or commentary. Parallels and similarities flow along much like extended similes. Whatever the vehicle chosen, the goal is so to involve the audience that they are moved to sense identity with the biblical character or experience or both, affirming the message in their total being. Our next task, then, is to set definitions and requirements for these vehicles of meaning or genres, describing their use in the planting and watering of faith.

Whatever the genre or genres selected, the first requirement for a sermon in my culture is a biblical text, and I highly commend it to preachers everywhere. This text may be chosen from the pericope where the narrative or other genre is found, or it may be in material about the life of the biblical character sketched. It may be in a verse of a psalm used as a stream of consciousness. In rare cases the text may be found in a biblical setting remote from the story, and still rarer may be the story that is memorable but contains no single sentence for textual purposes. Whatever the case, there ought to be a succinct, positive, biblical verse stating the central, controlling idea to be recorded (God willing) in the hearers' intuitive tapes for expression in the hearers' daily living.

This use of biblical texts achieves the goal that hearers of the Word be equipped with a repertoire of quotable gut beliefs: texts by which their very lives are sustained and ordered in the same way exemplified by Jesus and mentioned at the beginning of chapter 1. An elaboration of this crucial function of texts can be found in my work *Soul Theology* (pp. 2-4). Suffice it to say that when the whole person is reached, the whole person is nourished and strengthened. The goal is the wholehearted embrace of a biblical affirmation, to the extent that life is sustained and, in a helping sense, governed by it.

The use of the term "tapes" in connection with these quotable gut beliefs should perhaps be explained in more detail. Our intuitive responses to various experiences are like tapes played deep down in consciousness. If in early life we formed a habit of believing that the planet was safe, and God was caring for us, that amounts to a tape. In a crisis, we tend to "play" it again and live by that same habit of trust. If a child was mistreated or poorly cared for, that child will have emotional habits or tapes of fear and distrust. The negative experiences of fear need to be re-recorded or over-recorded with worship experiences of faith. If we are caught up in story-experiences of faith, or sing songs of great faith, we may be able to overcome the negative tape and establish habitual attitudes of positive trust in God.

This suggests the second requirement, which is that the speaker establish a clearly defined goal among the hearers, stated in behavioral terms. My calling it a "controlling idea" hints at a cognitive purpose. And it will of course be necessary to "show" truth or to teach ideas, but the bottom line is the behavior of the total person, not merely the understanding or assent. If the preacher does not know what God wants hearers to *do* about their fear or selfishness, how will the hearers ever be moved to go or grow or do? Paul said something about how people need a certain sound on the trumpet (I Cor. 14:8). Without the pompous pointing of fingers or the overkill of too much admonition (if indeed we use any "we-oughts" or "we-musts"), the goal is to motivate and empower behaviors such as trust and honesty and caring.

When the text and purpose are properly matched, the next requirement is that, regardless of the art form chosen, the material used must be full of living details. These bring the hearer aboard, or into the experiential encounter. This happens, as we have said, because of self-recognition and personal identification born of familiarity. Details bring "living color" to the communication and draw the hearer into the experiential matrix.

This experience is induced best when the preacher has already identified with the material and recounts it in an eyewitness mode. Some of these details come from the biblical record, and many will result from study of commentaries and encyclopedias. This must be coupled with inspired imagination. Often these details were originally condensed out of the Bible accounts, because of the familiarity with detail which was assumed to prevail commonly among the hearers of the oral tradition. Our providing the details is like putting the common substance called water back into the powdered milk. They are not the very same "water" or details that were removed, but they are so similar that the result is a very accurate portrayal. So because the preacher has envisioned the Patmos experience with "eyewitness" detail, the hearer can also.

Now to the art forms or genres—the vehicles of meaning—all of which will be examined closely in part 2, in separate chapters.

THE NARRATIVE

The narrative in the sermon can be defined like any other good story, except that it is told with the purpose of winning souls to Christ, helping them to grow, and motivating them to serve. The standard components of a story are required: setting, cast, plot, conflict, and resolution. The latter is timed carefully for the end, to sustain suspense. Narrative sermons should be at least as engaging or entertaining as other stories, since the opposite is not "educational" or "doctrinal" but boring. Ordination is no license to bore audiences. The sermon will not be heard and heeded without the engaging tales and images which make it come alive.

Good narration is required throughout in order to achieve the behavioral purpose, of course with subtlety. This is called *focus*. It requires that the issue in the text and purpose be the same issue as that of the conflict in the narrative. The protagonist, who takes the principal role in both the conflict and the resolution, also must embody the area of growth on which the sermon is focused. Thus, when the hearer naturally identifies with the story's main character, he or she vicariously participates in the same conflict, gains the same wisdom, and celebrates the same victory or resolution. This celebration I have called *ecstatic reinforcement* of the truth portrayed and the growth sought. Like the parables of Jesus, the point and purpose are premeditated.

For artistic purists, this may appear to corrupt the art of narration, to achieve a "utilitarian" purpose. They would argue that art ought to be for art's sake. This venerable Western shibboleth is found in no other culture of which I know, and it is not even truly practiced among the elitists who espouse it. *All* powerful literature has a driving motivation behind it; the author is always involved in projecting a message, consciously or unconsciously. Many years ago, in a graduate seminar on world literature at a state university, a student protested vigorously the requirement that he read a book by Dostoevski. He charged that the school was an arm of the government, and that since the author was "preaching," it was a breach of the separation of church and state to require such to be read. The professor heard him out patiently and then responded: "Of *course* Dostoevski was preaching," he said. "But so was Tolstoy last week, and so was every other author we have read this semester. Your problem is that you generally agreed with the preaching of the others, or just didn't see what it was. You resent Dostoevski because he is preaching the cross, or redemptive suffering." Every storytelling preacher needs to know the meaning and purpose of the tales told, and to be sure that the focus is within the will of God for the uses of the gospel.

In other words, as will be elaborated later, the entertaining genre must be carefully employed to be sure that it conveys what is intended, and to avoid accidental espousal of some unknown and undesirable end and impact. The rule of focus is that the issue or impact be the same in the text and purpose, and that the protagonist embody this issue, gaining over it the same victory urged in the text and desired in the hearer. It follows, of course, that the celebration must be about that victory or resolution of conflict.

This demanding but fruitful rule of focus will apply to a less rigorous extent to the other genres, with exceptions. (Cf. p. 47 for other exceptions.) When Jesus is the protagonist, it is not realistic to expect hearers literally to identify. Nobody will seriously expect to calm the sea or raise the dead, as did Jesus. These stories beget faith born of admiration and trust rather than identification. In the John 8 story of the woman taken in adultery, the Pharisees are one set of possible learners, but, again, the audience will not identify with persons so negatively portrayed. Unlike the prodigal son, there is no angle by which they can be described sympathetically as perhaps merely fallible, like us. So the hearer must celebrate Jesus' grace and wisdom under fire, and, it is hoped, internalize also the lesson of not throwing stones and not being judgmental in the bargain.

One other word must be said here; there is a sense in which personal testimony may be thought of as narrative. No doubt autobiographical stories are a form of narration, but they are so distinctive a story type as to justify a separate genre. One could wish that all stories were told with the same power. Personal testimony may well set the standard for all narratives, in the vividness of detail and the familiarity and identification of the speaker with the action. But there are other criteria, so testimony will be treated later as a separate genre.

THE CHARACTER SKETCH

Akin to the narrative is the character sketch, focused on a biblical personality, with details drawn from a wider scriptural base. (One may also do sketches of religiously significant personalities not found in the Bible.) In the biblical personality category, Paul provides a good example. He admonished thankfulness in all things in I Thessalonians 5:18. In Romans 8:28 he wrote a classical affirmation of the doctrine of Providence. In either case, with almost no material in the

Bible context for developing the sermon, one could do a sketch of Paul's life. It would feature examples of how his life clearly exemplified such a startling rule or principle as being thankful *all* the time. One could time the impact of the sketch to move to a celebrative conclusion, all the while helping the congregation to identify with Paul, and following the rules of focus. The lives of Abraham, David, Sarah, Peter, Priscilla, and many others offer great possibilities for fascinating biblical life sketches that are both effectively purposeful and powerfully timed and engaging.

THE GROUP STUDY

The genre called group study is parallel to the individual case study or character sketch above. It can deal with a whole people such as Israel, or a single congregation, such as the First Church of Corinth. Paul's letters reveal many interesting, folksy, and familiar issues there. Like the character sketch, in which the preacher should appear veritably to have grown up with the subject, the group study requires the preacher to seem to speak from the familiarity of a former member. In both cases, the point is that this conveys both the speaker's intimacy with details and personal identification with the action. The rules of focus apply in this case to a *group's* behavior, but the individuals find self-recognition in the group. Congregations in stress will be far better served by group studies with details, for instance, from II Corinthians, than by the negative fussing from the pulpit which is all too well known in churches with tensions. And whole families caught in a bind between a majority culture and a minority culture can take heart from a study of the family in which Timothy grew up.

THE DIALOGUE

Now to the dialogue, which often occurs within sermons, to great effect. The biblical accounts may appear at times to be close to verbatim, but in real life they were probably much longer. Most often one will have to enlarge on them by means of hard study and inspired, creative imagination. To achieve a credible length, one has to enlarge upon Jesus' talk with Zacchaeus at dinner (Luke 19:1-10), or Paul's words to the suicidal jailer at Philippi (Acts 16:26-28). Whether the dialogue is sermon length or, as is more likely, shorter, the rules of focus apply in general. That is, one has to know with which of the speakers the hearer is to identify, and how that hearer is to grow after listening to the account of the encounter. Full sermon length, or used within other story material, the dialogue is one of the easiest and best ways to brighten up a sermon and increase attention. Good conversation is always engaging, and provides for ease of identification and substantive growth toward the new person in Christ. Chapter 8 includes a sermon whose basic structure involves an extended imaginary dialogue with David.

THE MONOLOGUE OR TESTIMONY

Two kinds of monologue offer powerful ways of making the gospel come to life in the mind and soul of the hearer: the well-known personal testimony and the relatively new monologue in which the speaker impersonates a biblical character, with or without costume. A preacher announces, "My name is Mary of Magdala. You folks call me Mary Magdalene," or "My name is Hosea." The message then pours forth as a testimony from inside the mind and soul of the character indicated. It may be a life history or an account of the crucifixion from the perspective of one of the onlookers. Whoever is impersonated, the sermon comes with the vividness and feelings of a witness who bridges time and culture to bring the Bible to life here and now.

The personal testimony is perhaps the most powerful story one will ever tell, especially if it is about one's conversion. It has been mentioned already that personal testimony is a model in many ways: It offers visual clarity and vividness of detail and feeling, and audiences easily identify with it. But it requires some serious disciplines. Many preachers shun personal testimonies because they have heard so many conversion stories overworked manipulatively. A first rule, then, is to use conversion testimonies and other personal material sparingly. We preach Christ, not ourselves. A second rule would be that personal examples, even when used infrequently, should never lend glory to the speaker. Personally recalled stories in which we do not figure prominently need not be restricted, provided, of course, the action is far enough away in space and time to avoid breaches of confidence and privacy. Yet all one preaches, and especially the celebration, must be projected as from the very soul of the preacher. All of the gospel offered must be the obviously personal conviction of the speaker.

METAPHORS, SIMILES, AND ANALOGS

Jesus used a great many types of figures of speech in his preaching and teaching. The Parable of the Soils is a pure figure, with no plot or conflict (Matt. 13:3-9, 18-23; cf. similar passages in Mark 4 and Luke 8). It was effective because it was simply a familiar, striking parallel to experiences common in an agrarian society. Figures clarify and illuminate; they also motivate by providing identification. The writer of Hebrews includes all three (12:1-2)—clarification, illumination, and motivation—in a passage which lends itself handily for a sermon by using the figure of a foot-race: (1) Lay aside every weight; (2) run with patience; (3) look to Jesus, just as a good track runner must always look straight ahead; and (4) celebrate the joy!

I once preached a whole figure sermon on patience and longsuffering. Its text was Galatians 5:22, and it was built on parallels to the cooling system of an automobile. The sermon was preached on a Laymen's Sunday. Each aspect of an adequate cooling system was given a spiritual parallel. Hose clamps and normal maintenance were like regular prayer and disciplined devotional life. Thermostats, when worn out, misread conditions and caused cars to boil, as do overly sensitive (even paranoid) people. Foreign substances like dirt in the radiator were like selfishness clogging the human spirit. But not to worry. The Holy Spirit would overhaul your spiritual cooling system and give you patience. The effect of such details as freeze plugs and head gaskets was electrifying. These auto parts provided an all-too-rare means of male identification within the message. Well-chosen figures are vitally important.

Again, Jesus used many similes frequently introduced with words such as "the kingdom of heaven is like. . . ." Some of these employed figures, such as yeast or a seed, and some involved full-fledged narratives such as the one about the prodigal son. The Bible refers to all of them as parables. The varieties and uses of these figures of speech are set forth in greater detail in chapter 9. Suffice it to say that they enhance understanding of old ideas and free up new ideas, while also having great affective impact, by emotional identification and experiential encounter. And all of this is ultimately for the purpose of being used to move hearers closer to the new person in Jesus Christ.

THE STREAM OF CONSCIOUSNESS

Perhaps the least-known genre with high potential is what I call stream of consciousness. It amounts to getting inside the flow of thought of a person and identifying with her or his struggle for insight or peace or whatever. Most of the psalms lend themselves to this kind of sermon. Jesus himself is recorded as having worked his way through from despair to victorious faith by plugging, as it were, into the flow of a psalmist (Psalm 22), even as he hung from the cross. He started with "My God, my God, why hast thou forsaken me?" and, without the strength necessary to be heard, must have sung his way in his mind to the end, where the psalmist affirms the righteousness of God.

In the 139th Psalm, the writer moves through a marvelously honest array of moods to a final yielding cry: "And lead me in the way everlasting." Great mystics like Howard Thurman have used this genre with compelling power, but any sensitive and disciplined preacher can launch a congregation on a healing flow of consciousness. Some psalms hardly require more than a prayerful reading aloud. Indeed, it takes little more than a bit of poetry and some careful focus to make of many sermons as well as prayers an impressive stream leading to a truly experiential encounter with God and the Word.

It should perhaps be noted in passing that the monologue sermon, mentioned above, overlaps this category in many ways. Although the psalms were sung, in many cases they were essentially monologues put to music.

All these vehicles and others combine to give to the preacher a rich variety of approaches, both within a single sermon, and over a period of time, in many sermons. Just as it need never be said that the richness of the Bible has been exhausted, for it is limitless, neither need any preacher ever think that the possibilities for experiential encounter with God and the Word have been worked through. The task of the preacher is to become familiar and comfortable with the various styles or genres for addressing the intuitive, without which the totality of persons in the modern audience cannot be reached.

A word of warning before the topic of genre is concluded. There is no absolute need to find a *name* for the genre used, except in the classroom when samples of each are assigned. The issue is not *naming* the vehicle but *using* it to help the Word come alive—to be used of

God to help it form in human consciousness. Some of a given preacher's best moves may defy classification, partaking of the characteristics of several of the genre. You may be sure, however, that *no* abstract principle or doctrine ever comes to real life among the hearers without some concrete vehicle to bring it within reach and make it visible and felt or experienced.

The next concern is to fit all of this understanding about the begetting of faith and the use of literary genres into a plan for an actual sermon. We turn now to the outline.

OTHER EXCEPTIONS TO THE RULE OF FOCUS

Occasionally, Bible stories involve protagonists with whom we simply must not identify. Jesus did not intend for us to identify positively with the Unjust Steward (crooked accountant), Rich Man Dives, or the elder brother of the Prodigal Son. When we see ourselves in these people, it is only long enough to convict us and to motivate us to become more like Jesus. They stir in us their opposites, whether or not we make direct, open confession. But where is the positive embodiment of the goal with which to launch celebration?

The answer is to determine the theological field or field of meaning and to find a positive example of the compassion that Dives didn't have or the spiritual values that the rich farmer never had. Negative lessons then need to be paired with positive passages, so that there can be celebration relevant to the negative text's issue. The rich farmer, for example, might be paired with Paul in Philippians 3:12-13. Paul doesn't consider himself to have achieved very much of anything but looks to Jesus and celebrates the opposite of the rich farmer's attitude.

Some rules of thumb may be helpful:

1) "Negative" characters should rarely be used for more than the limit of one-third negative material.
2) Negative texts must always be yoked with positive texts.
3) The positive text for the pair must be chosen on the basis of the theological field.
4) The celebration must center on the positive text and character.
5) The hearers, sensitized by the negative, will identify with and celebrate the positive protagonist.

THE OUTLINE:
PLAN OF MOVEMENT

The immediate response of many students and pastors to all that I have said is, How does all this awareness of genres as vehicles of encounter (or formation in consciousness) translate into a sermon outline? The instant one leaves the beaten path, preachers get uneasy. They are accustomed to three points, some illustrations, and a poem; or they lean on a formula of exegesis, exposition, and application. This is understandable. We are far more comfortable as scriptural lawyers and philosophers than as homiletical artists, using all our exegesis and hermeneutics to form images in consciousness, using our skills with the Word under the power and control of the Holy Spirit. From outline as sequence-of-ideas we now move to outline as flow-*in*-consciousness.

The flow chart, outline, or plan of movement may become very threatening, in the sense that we are accustomed to a much simpler formula. That simpler formula demanded only abstract connections of ideas. Now we have to enter the life predicament of the hearers and sense how the sermon will flow in their consciousness. We will remain coherent, as we always were, but now we involve the whole person by speaking also to intuition and emotion.

A GOAL: SELF-RECOGNITION

Before considering the all-important sermon text and behavioral purpose, it may be well to ponder some details of a style of communication. This could influence the choice of texts and purposes, as well as the approach throughout the body of the sermon. We have cited vicarious experience as the process by which people alter intuitive tapes. They are "drawn into" the experiences of biblical characters, for instance, by identification. This occurs because of a kind of self-recognition, due to the vividness and living relevance of the description of these characters and their activities. One best moves persons to growth when the scriptural event is literally visualized by speaker and hearer in concrete terms, quite parallel to current experience.

There are at least two important values in this approach. The first and foremost is that self-recognition causes the Bible story to become the hearer's own story. The identification is not simply for the moment of hearing, but for life. The God who worked in Paul's and Joseph's life, for good, is seen and *felt* to be at work in the hearer's life, twisting and squeezing blessings out of the evil deeds that have been directed against "us." Romans 8:28, on the providence of God, is no longer a theoretical affirmation only. It is *owned* by the believer as a part of core belief. Thus, although faith may follow cogent, sequential arguments, it is formed in depth, if at all, on the basis of vicarious appropriation of the experience of Paul, or Joseph, or whomever.

Self-recognition, born of careful choice of adjectives, nouns, and verbs, also bridges time and makes the Bible into a current recording of timeless solutions, as well as predicaments. Joseph's oft overlooked tears in Genesis 50:17 are, in a sense, dateless. The tiny details unearthed by scholars have to be sifted, so that the emphasis is on existential similarities, not on the so-called problem of a gulf between an ancient culture and our own. David Buttrick says it well: "By imitating the consciousness of the story, we can avoid the then/now splits caused by first talking about the story, and then talking about our reactions. Instead, story and reaction are interwoven throughout the move" (*Homiletic,* pp. 360-61). The old dichotomy of abstract principles extrapolated somehow from antiquity, and then applied to modern life, is replaced by scriptural immediacy and responses, which are, as always, by the *whole* person. In some cultures, such as my own, this will have a very familiar ring. But David Buttrick has *named* the process and lifted it out of vague homiletical intuition, for the discipline and enrichment of preaching everywhere.

This sophisticated insight about the formation of things in consciousness is likewise quite familiar. It is precisely what has been happening through the centuries in the folk narrative traditions of supposedly primitive cultures, and in Black America's rich pulpit narrative tradition. It is no doubt what went on in the life of the Israelites, whose soul-shaping tales have come down to us in much of the Old Testament. Our style of communication, seeking identification and vicarious experience, then, is no wild-eyed new experiment. It was the universal style until academia judged it to be too simple and tampered with it. Our effort here is to reclaim the art.

THE SERMON TEXT

Let us now turn to the text out of which every sermon is born. A fitting marriage of biblical text and behavioral purpose—the goal of spiritual growth—must precede the birth of every sermon. Although either text or purpose may occur first in the planning process, the prior choice of purpose (usually because of legitimate pastoral concerns) must never be allowed to override the substantive integrity of the scriptural text. When text and purpose are well matched, a sermon will almost write itself.

The best texts for permanent personal growth are the brief, pungent ones, which are easy to memorize:

"In the beginning God created the heaven and the earth" (Gen. 1:1).
"Be not deceived; God is not mocked: for whatsoever a man soweth, that shall he also reap" (Gal. 6:7).
"For God so loved the world, that he gave his only begotten Son" (John 3:16).

Memorization has become unfortunately unfashionable, but persons who grow up in a culture where holy wisdom is memorized without formal efforts are indeed blessed. What a resource to be able to quote a verse of powerful scripture and not even remember when one learned it! The long-range goal of every pastor should be to equip the hearers with a repertoire of nourishing verses on which to depend in times of great stress, and with which to guide and interpret all of life. This collection of memorable passages would be a set of core beliefs or intuitive tapes, treasured for their trustworthiness and clarity as manuals or maps, and for their beauty. They would not constitute a code for conformity, but a searchlight for finding the path to abundant life.

This insistence on a brief, memorable sermon text cuts across a number of venerable habits and traditions. Perhaps the greatest of these is what some folks refer to as "expository preaching"—homiletic commentary on a Bible passage, verse by verse. It assumes that hearers must become cognitive Bible scholars and then Christians. Running commentary is marvelously valid in some pericopes, where scripture has a naturally focused flow, with ready-made moves toward a main purpose. This would be true of a sermon built around a narrative such as that of the Prodigal Son in Luke 15, or in the already mentioned use of the figure of footracing (Hebrews 12). Nevertheless, even here the sermon should have a brief, memorable text and a clear focus on a single behavioral purpose, such as "And when he came to himself . . ." (Luke 15:17), or "Let us lay aside every weight, . . . and let us run with patience" (Heb. 12:1).

Our text-focused pattern could be said to be "expository," in that the sermon always flows from a passage of scripture. The difference is that the narrower scriptural coverage gains in depth and sharp focus what it loses in scope. Every church-school teacher can "cover" all the different potential themes in a long passage thinly. But life-changing intensity comes from the fresh insights and motivating power of highly focused communication, even though one may use wide expanses of biblical context in the process. The aim is not so much to "cover" the Bible as to be used of God to regenerate and develop hearers in the direction of the new person in Jesus Christ. What is then "learned" of the Bible will be both better "known" and more faithfully followed, which is the purpose of expository preaching at its best. With the help of God, this must surely be what is meant by the Word not returning void.

Although all biblical passages may be said to contain some inherent signals concerning sermon flow, and structure, most do not have an obvious plan built in. That is, few pericopes will have adequately clear focus and timing of impact just from verse-by-verse exposition. Quite often, a variety of important ideas or texts will emerge. The hearers leave wondering what the main text was and, more important, what they are expected to do in response. *One* controlling idea and behavioral purpose is all any sermon can be expected to communicate with effectiveness, not great ideas from every verse. Most blessed is the preacher in whose ministry there is success with achieving even that one purpose most of the time. Thus it seems far better to attempt deep, experiential treatment of one main verse or text.

The sermon text itself always provides a purpose, and some hints of an organizing principle. In the vast majority of cases, the whole sermon should flow *from* the text; that is, very few sermons, if any, should allow the hearers to wonder from whence cometh this message, and by what authority? There are audiences, of course, who resent "authority" thrust upon them, but even they prefer a Bible basis for reflection, to the random ruminations of a preacher whom they rightly perceive to be a peer.

The most familiar justification for avoiding the early declaration of a text is seen in a biblical narrative sermon in which the text occurs toward the end of the tale. Such is the case with the Prodigal Son. Whether the punch line or text chosen refers to the son who "came to himself" (Luke 15:17) or the father who accepted him unconditionally (15:20), it occurs toward the end of the story. However, this is more the exception than the rule. Sermons flow *from* biblical passages, and they are best retained in memory by their association with a timeless text.

At the end of chapter 4 is a sermon, which may be said to be an extended "exposition" of its text. The homiletic moves are intentional combinations of exegesis and exposition, with additional materials to help in the *formation in consciousness* of the images and truths of the Word. The method used seeks to achieve the valid goals of traditionally expository preaching (homiletical points) by dealing with a feasibly brief text. This makes it possible to retain the goal of a single focus or purpose. Because of this approach, this sermon also perhaps comes closest in this book to a traditional "points" sermon. The critical difference has to do with formation in consciousness, as opposed to emphasis on argument.

THE BEHAVIORAL PURPOSE

Second only to the scriptural text is the sermon's behavioral purpose. Every sermon will have a controlling idea and require *some* intellectual growth or increased understanding, but maturity of attitude and behavior—deep trust, with willing obedience—is the central objective. It is often difficult to decide what a proper purpose for a given sermon might be. Two guidelines apply. The purpose should embody the action demanded by the biblical text, and it should reflect the preacher's "gut" motivation for writing the sermon, even though the idea may have been negative. The challenge is to convert a negative motivating idea to a positive behavioral purpose that flows out of the text.

The hearers are always the actors. The desired behavior may be for them to grow in forgiveness, honesty, unselfish service, or commitment to labor for peace or against world hunger. For example:

"To be used of God to move the hearers to trust God when they face financial crises."
"To help the congregation feel and affirm their self-worth or esteem as children of God."

The almost universal first urge is to say that the purpose is "to show . . .," which indicates a manifestly cognitive rather than behavioral ultimate intent. This urge seems a lofty purpose and a worthy work, but at center it is inadequate. Some examples of this urge are:

"To show that God is omnipotent, all-powerful."
"To teach the congregation that God is love."

People do need to be shown, of course, that God is omnipotent and loving. The ultimate goal, however, is not what the preacher will *say* about it but what they will *do* about it in their everyday lives. The stated purpose must deal with their dependence on and trust in God's power or love.

Because this purpose is so rarely framed in behavioral terms, it might be good to explain why intellectual growth is only secondary, before enlarging on what a purpose is and how it works in a sermon. Although the hearer must gain some understanding, faith is not sight, and not resident in the rational aspects of consciousness. It is those aspects of personality where faith *is* resident, and where behavior is the fruit, which require the most work. To make a sermon logical is easy; to give it impact experientially takes far more skill and imagination, as well as the aid of the Holy Spirit.

Meanwhile, reason cannot be simply ignored. Intellectual reflection may clear the way for faith to be born. Reason may cause faith to grow and gain strength *after* the gut conviction has been born in the believer. However, the joy born of reasonableness simply adds to gut certitude, once it is begotten. When one can say that it all makes sense now, already extant faith flourishes. This is equally true when one looks back on an experience of deliverance seen to be providential. Of course, the sectors of consciousness never operate in complete independence, and the exclusion of reason from the nurture of faith would be a foolish excess. However, the primary purpose is still a behaviorally defined trust, with concomitant obedience; the purpose is much more than mere understanding, as much that is to be desired.

The following is a graphic representation of the *whole* of consciousness. The diagram indicates the specialized sectors, without any clearly defined separation. There are other models, but the strength of this figure lies in its insistence on interacting or interlocking wholeness.

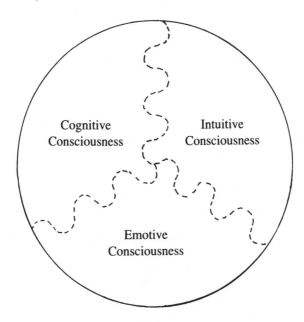

Although science has fairly well-defined evidence of different functions being performed in different sectors of the brain, there is no verbal access that can focus on one sector to the complete exclusion of another. Every time we preach, we preach to the whole person, our options being limited to emphasis on one or two, as opposed to the other two or one.

A rule of thumb for clarification of holistic purpose in sermon preparation is to ask, Am I struggling to get a point across or am I working at a flow in consciousness which will be used to beget trust and change behavior? Another way to put it is, Do I see and feel what I'm talking about, or am I myself obsessed with clever, scholarly data and abstract ideas?

Now, one other word on the choice of a behavioral purpose: It facilitates focus to a degree which exceeds all normal expectations. That is, awareness at every point of an affective (as opposed to a solely cognitive) purpose seems to make sound choices of material easier. It gives sermons a concentration of power uncommon if not impossible with communications aimed primarily at intellectual enlightenment.

As author-originator of this rule (so far as I know), I myself am amazed at the advantages encountered when I follow this somewhat surprising principle, which emerged uninvited in the sermon lab. I have also experienced the reverse when tempted to violate this still strange statute.

My courage to advance it so insistently comes partly from an experience with a Hollywood producer. On request, I wrote six proposed segment scripts for a television series on the African American church. The producer's rejections were based on what I finally saw to be my failure to follow for TV a rule exactly like my very own standard of narrowed focus for sermons.

The strongest support for a behavioral purpose stems from the fact that Jesus' teachings seemed concentrated on the *"observing"* of all the things he had commanded (Matt. 28:20), rather than on knowledge, assent, or verbal confession. He said it even more plainly in the Parable of the Two Sons (Matt. 21:28-32). The son who verbally refused but obeyed was far to be preferred to the son who said yes and did not follow through. The Parable of the Last Judgment (Matt. 25:31-46) is perhaps the ultimate example of behavioral purpose.

THE BODY OF THE SERMON

With the choice, then, of a text and a compatible behavioral purpose, the shape of the outline and the flow of the sermon may be well on their way. If one is sensitive to the text and the Spirit, this choice will dictate the mode of the encounter and determine the relevance and uses of various aspects of the exegetical studies. In fact, after that, the moves of the sermon will emerge naturally. Hebrews 12:1-2, already mentioned, is exemplary. The purpose would be to move hearers to patient persistence in the Christian life. The basic moves might be:

	(1) to lay aside unnecessary weights
(using the figure of	(2) to run with patience
track competition)	(3) to look to Jesus
(a perfect celebration)	(4) for the *joy*, and Jesus is set at the right hand of God

Not every text is so suggestive, however, even though every text worth preaching should have some of this kind of clarity of vehicle and direction. One of the most gripping examples ever written of elaboration on the minimal details of a biblical figure of speech was recently republished in the *American Baptist Quarterly* (vol. 6, no. 1, March 1987). Brother Carper, an ex-slave exhorting in the state of Missouri in the 1840s, was recorded from memory by a White Methodist minister. The sermon was from the figure of the "shadow of a great rock in a weary land" (Isa. 32:2). The moves came from his vivid visualization of a man in a sand storm. He described it so graphically and portrayed the "race" to safety behind the rock so dramatically that the whole audience shouted in relief when the last pilgrim barely reached the shelter ahead of the storm. The ex-slave preacher's effectiveness was in his ability to help hearers see and literally experience the text's force, which lay in the graphic and soundly imaginative enlargement of its figure.

Just as the choice of genre is often indicated by the text or purpose, so in turn the flow chart is determined by the genre, as just occurred with the figure of a rock shelter in a storm. For instance, the *narrative* genre will need the usual elements (handily listed on a sermon worksheet or checklist): setting, plot-conflict, protagonist and cast, resolution, and celebration. A worksheet might also include special angles and details for vividness. The flow itself will be stated in principal stages of action, like acts of a play, which now are often referred to as "moves," the term we shall use here. From a distance, these moves may look like the old outline of abstract points or general statements, but they are radically different. They are movements in consciousness made real by the supply of details crucial to the development of the plot. These details also help people get aboard and find identity in the action. Needless to say, they also grip the hearers' attention. Whatever the story or parable, its genre as narrative will set the course of the flow, the "acts" of the drama, or the outline.

The Parable of the Prodigal Son would narrate well with these moves:

Introduction (optional with stories; they introduce themselves).
1) The son feels powerless and unrecognized at home, so he asks for his inheritance and goes forth to seek his fortune.
2) The fine line between productive public relations and wasteful drain of resources is overlooked, and he lands in dire poverty before he is able to establish anything like a career or business.

3) The shock of having to eat with the pigs helps him come to himself and make a good decision to repent and go home to his father.
4) His father forgives and receives him, and holds a party to celebrate his return.

Note that the moves involve statements of consciousness applicable to any age, and that the moves constitute an adequate summary of the story. Note also that move 1 reverses much tradition by luring the hearer to *identify* with the prodigal. Only then will the hearer be motivated to "return home," which is the purpose.

One will need roughly similar stages of movement in other genres, even without the facets of the footrace figure in Hebrews or obviously structured conflict in a parable. There has to be purposeful flow in the sketch, case, or stream of consciousness. The stages of the story parallel the acts of a play, and the movements in the other genres can be called stages of development, against a background of an unpersonified opposition or conflict of some sort. The streams of consciousness in the Psalms are not inhibited in this regard; they call an enemy an enemy and cry out against him before God. Whatever the style of stating the undercurrents against which the movement struggles, the point is that the sermon must have a plan of development which moves with focus on the purpose and with carefully calculated timing.

Worksheets for a single narrative sermon and a sermon with moves from within the meaning of the text appear at the end of chapter 4. Note that even with the powers attributed to the genres studied, the fact is that they will often be employed for only single moves, rather than for the whole sermon. The goal of each move within the sermon is to help the gospel to form in consciousness. Even if there is no identifiable genre, or if the genre used is so brief as hardly to deserve the name, the purpose of that move is to make a portion of the gospel real in all sectors of consciousness. The one ruling concern is to help persons visualize and relate holistically by any means at the preacher's command, be it word picture, figure, tale, or whatever.

At this point, realism on my part requires a kind of interim ethic in the matter of outlines. It is all too manifest that many readers who read and heed will still find it very difficult to move from the old pattern. In fact, I am not altogether innocent on this issue myself. So here are some suggestions for a start in the direction of the moves for an ideal sermon-encounter.

First, every sermon except a one-story sermon should have a brief, pointed, and gripping introduction. One-story sermons will draw attention merely by signaling to the audience that there is a tale coming up. All the world loves a narrative told well. Apart from this natural attention-getter, one will need to raise a gripping conflict (issue), with a compelling way to open it up, to get the attention of the audience. A good introduction gains the audience's attention and focuses it on the issue at hand, all in a very few sentences.

Once the issue or malady of spirit is lifted up, the suspense should rise in anticipation of an answer, which is assumed to come from the unfolding of the text offered. One needs to be very careful, however, that one does not offer both issue and answer at this point. A perennial failing of even very experienced pastors is to tell it all in the first few sentences—to preempt suspense, or "telegraph the punch," as we say in class. For example:

"Our text this morning commands us to love our neighbors." (Unless the next words are "How on earth can we do that?" the sermon is over.)

"Whether we like it or not, the Word of God commands us to put the kingdom of God first in our priorities." (Needs to start where the hearers are and leave them some of the final answer to anticipate.)

"Jesus is the answer to *all* the world's problems." (O.K., let's go home.)

Once the topic or text is out there, let the grasp of its significance grow in stages. Premature answers keep the sermon from achieving the impact possible with proper timing.

The next step for me in the development of a sermon outline is always the exegesis. Sometimes, as in the Hebrews 12 example above, the exegesis is the whole sermon. It could almost be called a stream of consciousness, as the preacher and the hearers grapple with the text. The quest for meaning involves the seeker in stages of experience, which become the moves of the sermon. When the preacher comes to the final, victorious stage, the hearers have shared and identified with both the struggle and the reward of spiritual growth. One cannot arbitrarily rule out the old pattern of exegesis followed by the standard "points illustrated" or principles applied. But even here the preacher's deep involvement should keep it from being a dry and sterile cognitive exercise. The process can be made to produce encounter if the preacher is deeply involved, and if the details and illustrations are true to life and lively. The goal so clearly preferable is to create a flow of thought and vicarious experience, which runs in and with the scripture, rather than to encourage hearers to think abstract thoughts about the scripture.

Important to remember is that outlines are not an instrument invented by professors to torture students. They are road maps to help the preacher arrive at the destination, with all the flock aboard. If one rebels against an outline written prior to the first draft, and prefers to let the Spirit flow in a gush, fine! That is a matter of preference. But if one tries to identify a coherence of flow in the gush and finds none, one need not expect the audience to make any more sense of the sequence than did the person who wrote it. Often, we need to cut and paste our first-flush inspirations, saving some for a later sermon in which they will fit better. If there is no outlining discipline engaged in either before or after the first draft, pray that ye think so architectonically that ye have no need of such. Few there be whose thought is fully organized, and they are happy to confirm it by at least checking the flow pattern for coherence and focus. Outlines are an indispensable discipline for preachers who want the audience to follow along with the sermon and in the flow, to encounter the Word in depth.

Omitted thus far has been the final and, in many ways, the most important element of the flow chart, plan of movement, or outline for the sermon: the celebration. Everything leads up to this peak of ecstatic reinforcement, as we have suggested. We turn now to a whole chapter on this long overlooked and climactic component of the preaching event.

CHAPTER 4

THE SERMON CELEBRATION

The contribution I want to make here farthest from the beaten path of academic homiletics is this emphasis on celebration. One might suspect the accent on emotion to be an equally fresh insight, but only if one had not read other recent writers on homiletics. What is proposed here is a matter of taking the new-found acceptance of emotion (not emotionalism) to its logical conclusion, with a finale of feelings which parallels the finale of the action and ideas. Instead of simply winding down and taking a seat, the preacher-performing artist engages in a final, triumphant or celebrative expression of the theme or the resolution of the conflict or issue. As we have already proposed, the hearer should be glad about the gospel in a manner comparable to that of the audience at the final act of a drama or the final movement of a symphony.

The very mention of such a phenomenon may stir up the fearful specter of the return of the bizarre behaviors at Cane Ridge, or at holy roller revivals in the early twentieth century. Now, of course, that might not be so bad, after all, for the sawdust trails and shouting Methodists are an important and positive part of the roots of all of us. Much can be offered, however, to guarantee against the excesses that brought our earlier spontaneity to an untimely demise among the major brands of American Protestantism. When the final reaction against the Billy Sunday level of emotion occurred, we threw out the baby with the bath. The celebration proposed here is designed to get the baby back. This time the presence of the Spirit and the ecstasy of the Good News can be as authentic and "respectable" as they were when judges and bankers were won to Christ by the dozens, in the "Burned Over Territory" of up-state New York, under Charles G. Finney. To accomplish such a renaissance of authentic, holistic expression in sermons, and to establish gut affirmation of biblical truths, we will need to accept and follow some relatively simple and manifestly common-sense criteria. For our purposes here, these guidelines will be focused on sermon celebration.

CELEBRATION AS RELEVANT EMPOWERMENT

For some, celebration may seem to eliminate the ending of sermons on a prophetic or "challenging" note. This may come as something of a surprise, in the light of the emphasis placed here on a behavioral purpose. The absence of negative, highly critical exhortation at the conclusion raises the suspicion of escapist or quietistic pietism. This is possible only on the basis of a surface reading.

The facts are quite to the contrary! One can be prophetic on a very positive note as readily as on the opposite. The word of Isaiah, prince of the prophets, concerning the Prince of Peace, is patently positive (9:6). The preacher who is dominantly negative in the prophetic role should be warned that this leaves very little priestly potential for healing and empowerment. In a free church tradition, he or she may even be granted no role at all. It could be that Christ came, as one professor put it, "to comfort the afflicted and to afflict the comfortable," but he was not called and paid by them.

All humankind is now afflicted, however, and there is good reason not to accept ministry restricted to the "spanking" of those presumed to be privileged. That is, unless one finds an unlikely congregation of spiritual masochists. All humankind has problems, from finding table grapes to finding peace and eliminating world hunger and deadly atmospheric pollution. No one is beyond the need for the healing and empowerment of the relevant affirmations from the gospel.

Henry Sloan Coffin used to warn his preaching classes not to use the pulpit for a whipping post. One has to be sick to welcome such a ministry. Unresolved guilt, no matter how it is generated, is not saving; its brief and only role is as prelude to the reception of grace. By itself and held over time, it becomes a sickness called guilt neurosis. Healthy hearers will not permit this indefinitely. Miles Mark Fisher, the late pastor of the White Rock Baptist Church in Durham, and a professor at Shaw University, put it another way when he warned his students, "Don't *use* your influence until you *get* it," and this applies in particular to prophetic preaching.

Even more important, people *do* what they *celebrate;* they may also do what they are browbeaten against doing. The topics about which we admonish may register in deep consciousness, but the negatives do not. A lengthy diatribe against any one sin in the catalog of sins amounts to a kind of reverse-impact advertisement. It places the sin in consciousness—puts it on the hearer's mind. So, like the demons swept out in Jesus' Parable of the Empty House, negative pre-dominance may sweep clean (Matt. 12:43-45; Luke 11:24-26), but without the affirmative emphasis, a dangerous vacuum is left in the moral makeup of the hearer.

In other words, more than a third of a sermon devoted to don'ts and other negatives, with no positives and celebration to "fill the house," leaves a hearer worse off than before. Although a sermon may have to include a clear description of the sin involved, the less negativity, the better. To draw listeners aboard, sermons must generally avoid starting out to be critical of the hearers. To give the Word ecstatic reinforcement, the sermon must also end on an affirmative note. People cannot actually be glad about what does not exist, or what is wrong, or what ought to be, no matter how justified the criticism may be. The surprising good news is that celebration is the best way to motivate people to *do* the will of God.

Thus, celebration is not to be mistaken for exhortation, even though it may actually bring the same result. The concluding "challenge" so often heard is not as great a motivator as being glad about God's will and work in that same area of the Kingdom. One is moved to wish to take part in bringing it to reality. There may be exceptions, but they partake of both celebrative affirmation *and* a kind of challenge. For instance, one may use a song that declares determination to follow Jesus, but it is celebrating both acceptance of a challenge *and* healthy confidence in the singers' capacity to stick to their vows. The Epistle to Timothy urged him to reprove, rebuke, and exhort, and all of these must be done, but in proper ratios and at the proper time, which is *not* the celebration.

One critical distinction needs mentioning here. There is a huge difference between "fiery mad" and "fiery glad." One should beware of assuming that the emotional expressiveness of some is celebration. Only *positive* truths about God through Christ give healing and empowerment, causing great rejoicing and praise. The more people rejoice about the goodness and faithfulness of God, the more they establish that joyous quality or atmosphere in the psychic space of their inner lives, regardless of outer chaos. Modern people affirm this approach generally, but they have subtle cultural inhibitions about putting it into actual religious expression. Yet one could go so far as to say that it is spiritually dangerous to repress one's joy. Preaching's accentuation of the positive Good News should help hearers to be liberated from this dead hand of the cultural past, as well as to seek by faith and work to liberate the oppressed.

So although challenge is not the same thing as rejoicing, celebration does not take the activist edge off the experiential encounter. One is more apt to work for justice after celebration of the justice of God, or one's high place in God's plan, than to respond to a pointed rebuke. People are motivated more by love and joy than by fear or even by negatively "prophetic" utterance.

A THEOLOGY OF CELEBRATION

Once the "we ought" is removed from the "climax," the question arises about how much one needs exhortation anywhere in the sermon, and to what extent the lack of exhortation softens the gospel and cheapens grace. The minute one sees that the often used word *gospel* means Good News or glad tidings, it should be apparent that the traditional sermons of Protestant orthodoxy have been entirely too judgmental, critical, and characterized by bad news. One dare not deny that Jesus came to judge the earth, but the main arena of that judgment is in the future and not the past or present. If the gospel is Good News, there is a sense in which the sermon should be somewhat celebrative from the very start. There ought not to be an exclusively intellectual and solemn section, after which comes the second or happy part. It is not that a preacher ought to be a stand-up comedian, or a perpetual teller of humorous stories. Inevitably there will be sad illustrations and stern warnings. Yet the experientially involving sermon must come from a preacher who has already tasted and experienced the Word of God, and shows a pleasant countenance because of it. That preacher dare not be against letting some of this joy be seen and felt by contagion, throughout most if not all of the sermon, and in increasing amounts.

It is just good theology to insist that the tone of the Good News be joy and celebration. Questionable for centuries has been the theology which kept people off balance and manipulable by asking them to sing of themselves as "wretches" ("Amazing Grace") and "worms" ("Alas, and Did My Savior Bleed"). Of course, appropriate humility is absolutely indispensable. And, of course, television ministries that urge the self-affirmation which promises riches and self-indulgence are abominations. But the Good News of the grace of God embraces and affirms humble believers, healing and empowering them for service.

The cry that celebrative Good News is cheap grace is utterly without justification. It is supposedly too easy on iniquity and too soft on sinners. Somehow sinners should have no right to all this joy and celebration. The proper countenance of a transgressor should be dour. But it was precisely for his denial of this misreading of the Kingdom that Jesus was accused of hanging out with winebibbers. And, of course, his first public appearance was at a wedding celebration in Cana of Galilee.

It may be important to know who raises the cry of cheap grace. If it comes from one whose self-image is that of a co-offender, the good news is that found in I John 1:8-9, which declares that the penitent are forgiven and cleansed, whereof they may be suitably and openly celebrative. If the critical cry comes from the self-righteous, the Word has not been heard in the first place. If the cry comes from the purely abstract motives of a theologian, the weight of theological tradition must be overcome by an overwhelming encounter of the sort herein described. The behavioral fruits of such an experience in the first and last instances would clearly deny that the grace was cheap; rather it would have been life-changing, in the direction of empowerment for service *and* abundance of joy.

Another theological objection might deal with the manner in which the artistic demands in the designs of these experiential encounters might seem at times to override the purity of the Word. Re-arrangements for behavioral effect might actually alter meanings, it might be argued. Let it be understood that the artist and the theologian are the same person, and must never be in actual conflict. This will be dealt with in more detail in chapter 5, in the section on the universal requirements of timing in all the genres.

A final theological consideration has to do with the sensitivities of those prone to react to celebration as too sure of itself intellectually. They think of this joy as requiring the celebrative preacher to be downright doctrinaire. They think that sermons could and should be open-ended—concluded with a question. This might be true for audiences with great security of all kinds, and with unlimited self-confidence as they face modern life. However, my experience suggests that the whole world is hurting in one way or another. They may resent doctrinaire hard-liners and pompous know-it-alls, but they want a word from the Lord. There are enough questions around for everybody, without coming to church to collect some more. The only questions capable of reaching the pain will be manifestly rhetorical.

Then the Word audiences seek must mean so much to the preacher that he or she is manifestly glad about it. Public jubilation should not be reserved for touchdowns and home runs. Authentic gospel feasting begets its own irresistible celebration; to hold it back or inhibit it is to lose the joy itself, along with the whole message. It is of more than passing significance that the Shorter Catechism of the Presbyterian tradition declares that "the chief end of man is to glorify God and to *enjoy* him forever." A sermon to the whole person demands a celebration that speaks to and through the emotive, bathing the Word in firm certitude and great, unforgettable rejoicing. This is theology at its best.

CELEBRATION AS SUMMARY AND FOCUS

The first requirement of celebration, technically speaking, is related closely to the theological. The substance of the message must be summarized, directly or symbolically, and lifted up in joy and praise. Since one cannot primarily *cerebrate,* digesting significantly new material, and *celebrate* at the same time, celebration is giving thanks for the spiritual feast already received. It is not another course to be consumed.

This is not to suggest a literal summation, such as is used in formal and academic documents. It is simply to suggest that the main purpose be lifted up in unforgettable refrain, with or without its subsections, if there be any. Whatever the style used, be it narrative, rhetoric, or whatever, the celebration expresses gladness about what God has done and is doing in the same area in which it is the purpose to engender growth. In other words, the affirmation celebrated must be the very same affirmation as that taught and experienced in the main body of the sermon. This may seem trite and overemphasized, but listening through the years has convinced me of the need to lift the issue once more.

Among the traditions having long practiced celebration, one of the cardinal sins has been referred to as "irrelevant climax." This sin finds preachers making sure that the celebration is powerfully moving, whether it relates to the purpose of the sermon or not. The "lesson" is taught, and then a stock celebration is pasted on. It may be a dramatically detailed account of one's own conversion. It may be a similarly vivid visit to the bedside or the grave of one's mother. Or it may be a patented and spectacular visit to the cross and the crucifixion. In every case, it grips the audience with readily recognized details. It "catches them up" in an unforgettable experience. The problem is that it virtually erases from memory the meat of the message. The body of a sermon is often best written after it becomes clear how the celebration will relate to the text and purpose. This helps to ensure that the main body will be written to flow into a celebration that focuses on the purpose.

The principal reason many veteran preachers perform these paste-on celebrations is that they have such a small repertoire of moving climaxes. Such preachers are predictable and redundant because they have not sought out the rich resources and challenging variety of celebrations in the Bible, as well as elsewhere. The "gravy" they seek could be as varied as the texts, if it were drawn from the "meat," as all good gravy is. Many texts have a celebration built right in, such as the Hebrews 12:2 text on the joy that was set before him, or the Luke 15:22-23 text on the feast held to celebrate the return of the prodigal son.

Given these criteria, the emotional qualities found in genuine celebration should be acceptable everywhere, since they perform the function we have called ecstatic reinforcement. These qualities and good imagery make the lesson unforgettable. People remember a good celebration even if they forget everything else. If the celebration is irrelevant to the main message, however, the recall will apply to the celebration only. If the celebration lifts up the message, the enhanced recall will apply to the whole message, by association. Thus the meaning of the message will be lastingly influential toward growth.

THE STYLE AND MATERIALS OF CELEBRATION

Having dealt thus far with the flow and form, the structures and meanings of celebration, we come now to the nuts and bolts of style and materials.

Many years ago I would have said that for celebration the sermon must move from analytical style and logical impressiveness to the flow and beauty of poetry. Although this is now obsolete, there is still more than a grain of truth in that statement. Authentic celebration requires poetic license; the task demands the free flow of joyous emotion. Powerful hyperbole, which would be quite out of place in the moves of the body of the sermon, is indispensable in the celebration for the purpose of lifting up symbolically the biblical truths earlier stated more directly. Altogether too many sermons end with quoting from hymns; however, the idea of using a poem of *some* sort is not far from the mark. Power and beauty of expression are required to ensure that the sermon will not just wind down or peter out.

Celebration is also very *personal*, in the sense that it has to involve the preacher's own emotions. The testimony of real experiences such as one's own conversion is a powerful catalyst for celebration. Like the hymns, it ought not to be overly repeated, but its joy is the most contagious thing I know of, and for obvious reasons. It offers the most vivid description in the entire repertoire of the preacher, and it refers to an experience with which all the saved can identify. One ought never to engage in what Henry Sloan Coffin used to call "ecclesiastical nudism" or a personal peepshow. But cold detachment and distance are equally inappropriate in the celebration, provided one does not engage in self-glorification. In between is a warm involvement that gives the glory to God and moves people to rejoice, and to grow in the process.

This movement of hearers is by contagion; people are led, not pushed, into genuine celebration. The first person into the waters of ecstasy should be the communicator of the Good News, which suggests a rigorous demand on the spiritual life of the preacher. The fact that celebration is personal, forces the preacher beyond the occasional, moving tale from personal life, to a perpetual obligation to be transparently authentic. This translates into some challenging applications. For instance, when a manuscript preacher is not familiar with his or her document, to the point of reading poorly, having had at least a week to prepare, how can that preacher expect hearers to gain from the sermon a joy that is celebrative? And if the Word is so powerless as to leave the preacher lackadaisical about it, how could anyone ever expect the congregation to celebrate on first hearing? The preacher should be both deeply sincere about, and especially familiar with, the celebration.

Under this necessity, there may arise a great temptation to engage in false enthusiasm, but this is not a feasible answer. It is utterly awesome to discover how accurately some of the laity read the preacher, and then God is not pleased either with sincere efforts to cover a lack of enthusiasm. Which could leave the preacher "winging it," with no help from the Holy Spirit. It is better to lay bare one's soul, in ways that express feeling, even if it is a feeling of frustration. There is only a fine line between this sort of thing and the ego trips sometimes seen among television preachers. However, the risk of unanimated celebrations is far greater. The truly dedicated and prayerful preacher can rely on the Holy Spirit to keep personal witness from one's depths within the bounds of cultural propriety and spiritual usefulness. Without self-glorification, the preacher must be as deeply emotional in the celebration of the sermon as in the flow of life at home or even in the ball park. It is good for the preacher to engage in spiritual self-discipline, which enhances expressiveness, as well as to tend the fires of the spirit in devotional life.

This brings back to mind the fact that personal testimonies are very vivid. The details are well known to the preacher, and the account is literally "eyewitness." Congregations celebrate best that which they have best visualized and experienced. The challenge is for the preacher to generate celebrations of equal authenticity with her or his conversion, from material of equally moving detail, although *not* autobiographical. The best verbal paintings as well as poetry should be saved for the celebration at the last. The joy they are used to stimulate is authentic, precisely because vivid detail begets an authentic and irrepressible expression of celebration, which is all still in the interest of the original behavioral purpose.

It has already been made clear that heightened rhetoric and poetic language are the material of celebration. Such expression is not appropriate when employed for minor topics, or in the main body of a sermon in which the celebration will then have to "top this." Rhetoric's force and beauty give the final drive to the behavioral purpose, and they also signal closure.

This heightened rhetoric *belongs* at the end, and it is not useful in the more logical and detailed communication in the body of the sermon. Embellished language is more suitable for the expression of deep feeling, or the symbolic projection of those things which surpass understanding. They do not negate reason; they simply go beyond the places we are capable of venturing to with logic.

In modern times, this rhetorical style has fallen on evil days in many circles. A friend of mine stormed from a convention hall muttering, "That was nothing but rhetoric, flights of rhetoric." He was leaving during the final sentences of a convention address by Martin Luther King, Jr. It had moved thousands of people, and was part of a historic ministry to the nation and the world. But my friend was a member of the generation that revolted against the rhetoric of evangelists and politicians, whose powers had not always been harnessed to high principle or scholarship. What my friend was doing was like eliminating all dynamite because some of it is used for purposes more destructive than road-building.

It is true that Martin Luther King's ''I Have a Dream'' speech (as well as many others) was unadulterated rhetoric, but its place in history is secure, alongside such great rhetoric as Lincoln's ''Gettysburg Address.''

The Bible has its own samples of great rhetoric. The end of the eighth chapter of Paul's letter to the Romans is a sweeping rhetorical tour de force. ''Who shall separate us from the love of Christ?'' His answer is awesome. The same can be said of his rhetorical devices in II Corinthians (4:7-10; 6:1-11). The combination of great affirmation and high rhetoric is nowhere better used than in the close of the Twenty-third psalm: ''Surely goodness and mercy shall follow me all the days of my life.'' Always in the forceful affirmative, and phrased to stir the very soul, these samples of rhetoric occur almost anywhere in the Bible. Ruth's declaration (1:16-17) is a most memorable sample of beauty, and Handel's ''Hallelujah Chorus'' thunders Revelation's (19:6 and 16) rhetorical affirmation of the final lordship of Christ. There are biblical jewels of rhetorical power lying everywhere, for those with sensitivity to respond.

A most common source of poetry today is the lyrics of great hymns of the church. These have the advantage of being familiar and of offering a means of congregational participation in the celebration, since they may be sung just after they have been recited. There is always the temptation to use them too often, but in moderation they are marvelous vehicles of celebration which involve the entire congregation. I can never forget the experience I had when I matched text, purpose, and celebration, as I preached from Philippians 4:11, of Paul's contentment in whatsoever state he was in. At the height of the celebration, I quoted Horatio Spafford's great hymn, ''It Is Well with My Soul.'' It hardly needed any special effort on my part, for when the congregation was given their opportunity to join in, they almost exploded in their moving expression of what had now become theirs, both lesson and celebration. To preach with inhibition while employing such rich rhetorical treasures is to rob the gospel of untold power and life-changing impact. It is better to cry victoriously with Joshua, ''As for me and my house, we will serve the Lord'' (24:15), than to plead with people for commitment. The immediate response of the Israelites was, ''God forbid that we should forsake the Lord, to serve other gods.''

Such is the impact of rhetoric addressed to the whole person. Those who have already identified with Joshua will go the distance—to join him and share his strength. The rhetorical artistry of folktales and oral tradition was always based on this wisdom about how to help people be what they ought to be. The folk-epic heroes were embodiments of the values and beliefs of their cultures. The Davids and Gideons of the Old Testament, as we have their records, were used in *teaching*. The Incarnation is a teaching *story* with great details. And we, today, can claim the power of the Word and its impact on behavior by means of preaching for the same kind of vivid experiential encounter, to the entire consciousness of the persons among whom we are called to serve.

There are a few other celebrative materials, such as epigrams and pithy, clever statements, which grasp attention and communicate profound affirmation with uncanny clarity and power. There is also the effective use of the figures and narratives and other genres already described in chapter 2. And there is the preacher's own spirit, facial expression, and tonal qualities, which serve as vehicles of contagious celebration.

As a means of exemplifying a typical application of all that has been suggested in chapters 2 and 3, here is a sermon of moves drawn from the exegesis-exposition of the text shown. The title of the sermon is "A New Model for Macho," and it was preached on the occasion of several "Men's Day" celebrations across the country. It was an effort to share the insights and growth that had taken place during a tour of Russian evangelical (Baptist) churches. The open Bibles in the hands of the hearers as the sermon begins add much to their identification with both the Word and the message, and help them to relate to an aspect of Paul not widely familiar.

A NEW MODEL FOR MACHO

Therefore I take pleasure in infirmities, in reproaches,
in necessities, in persecutions, in distresses for Christ's sake:
for when I am weak, then am I strong.
(II Cor. 12:10)

Introduction

A common cry of men through the centuries has been, "I am a man!" In so saying we have celebrated our strong muscles and sometimes stern characters. Some brag louder than others, and some are truer than others, but even the most mild Christian gentleman wishes to be known as a *man*. None of us enjoys being called a milquetoast or a wimp.

Now masculinity is part of what God planned for the human race, but let me offer a new and biblical model for macho. A *little* muscle flexing is O.K., but when we go overboard, we are at great risk. The world has thousands of sickly widows whose big, bad husbands died eight years younger than they will die. Men have heart attacks proving their super powers with too many jobs, and even being too rigorous in their recreation. The apostle Paul offers a strange but highly workable approach to this dilemma. It culminates with the words, "When I am weak, *then* am I strong." What on earth could this possibly mean? And how did he happen to say it in the first place?

Well, he was under the usual fire of false criticisms from the folks at Corinth. When you read the charges he had to defend against, you'll easily understand how he was tempted to defend himself with "the record," as it were. If you have your Bibles, please turn to II Corinthians 1:1. There Paul says that he is an apostle *by the will of God*. This may sound a little like bragging, but he is really fighting the rumor that only people who have seen Jesus in the *flesh* can be real apostles. In 3:1-2 he says, "*You* are *my* letter of commendation," again seeming to brag a little. Actually he is defending against the charge that he has no ordination papers, while lesser lights have epistles of commendation. In 5:13-14 he says, "Whether I be beside myself, it is to God . . . the love of Christ constrains me." It's easy to see here that somebody had said he was crazy, an unbalanced ecstatic. In I Corinthians 9:15-16 he has already defended against the charge that he is a "money hound." He flatly boasts that while ministers deserve their wages, "I *earn* my way!" Then he backs off and says that he preaches because he must, so it's nothing to glory about. That makes the next charge, in II Corinthians 10:10, hurt even more; they say he can write great letters, but he can't preach a drop. There is no worse charge against a preacher. His defense here in verse 18 leaves the glory and the homiletical evaluations to the Lord, but he is actually hurt.

Coming closer to our text, we find Paul accused of not having the real spirit. He is tempted to match visions with his critics. It is interesting to watch him as he struggles against this temptation. After all, he knew a man who was carried to the third heaven fourteen years ago, but he'd best not go into further detail. In fact, God gave him a thorn in the flesh, just to keep him from getting too carried away with his glorying. We have no idea what this thorn was, epilepsy or whatever. It was so great he prayed three times for deliverance, but God just told him that divine grace was sufficient for his need. So accepting this, Paul finally conquers the macho temptation to brag, and resigns himself to humble service, empowered and taken care of by God, who perfects our strength when we face our weakness. Paul decides that instead of glorying in whatever strengths he has, small or great, he will keep a low profile and let the power of Christ be manifest in his life. "When I am weak, that's when I am strong."

MOVE 1

Paul is saying that he is stronger *physically* when he honestly accepts his limitations. Thought by some to have been bandy-legged and smaller than average, Paul dares not overtax his frame; yet he does survive whipping and shipwreck. A big mouth could get him killed by the Roman military police.

Many a man has died crying "I ain't scared of you!" Several of my most boastful friends lie in relatively early graves for refusing to face their limitations. Yet one of the first deacons I worked with forty-five years ago is at church every Sunday and hearty at ninety-three. He thanks God for health and strength, and the steel grip of his handshake proves he has it. He has kept the strength he has by knowing its limitations and not overtaxing it.

MOVE 2

Then Paul, the thoughtful theologian of the early church, is saying that when he faces his *intellectual* limitations, God gives revelations beyond his fondest expectations. If he thinks he knows it all already, he will neglect to ask God for that which, as he says, "surpasses human knowledge" (Eph. 3:19 and Phil. 4:7). It is a terrible thing not to know and then not to know that you don't know.

One day during World War II a friend of mine and I were discussing an approaching ordination, while he worked away on a church roof. When he used a word I had never heard, I asked a few questions and wound up getting invited back to his study, miles away, to prove that he was correct. He shouldn't have come down off the roof, but he wasn't content to do it by phone later. To his absolute amazement, the word was not in a four-inch-thick Webster's dictionary. As he returned to his roof, he seemed ready to have a stroke, all because he had asserted his infallibility, instead of affirming his possible need for a dictionary. The more one knows, the larger is the boundary on which one is exposed to the unknown—and the greater is the awareness of weakness and what one doesn't know. *Then* are we mentally strong.

MOVE 3

Paul is perhaps most aware of his weakness *emotionally* and *spiritually*. He is in the habit of saying that he is the least of all the saints (Eph. 3:8 and I Cor. 15:9), having persecuted the church. He knows fully well that he does have a bad record. He actually admits that bragging about his visions is the height of foolishness (II Cor. 12:6). Yet it is just at this point that he is best suited to be used by God. Even if he is described in the worst terms, as accomplice to a murder, he is in company with Moses and David, both of whom were used mightily by God. When they were aware of their spiritual and moral weaknesses, exactly then were they given strength.

Human nature has not changed. Every preacher will tell you that when the sermon seemed a masterpiece, it somehow flunked. And when the pulpit was entered in fear and trembling, *then* was the Word given with surprising power. A lay couple in a great church rose to lead a memorial service. The husband was sweating profusely as his wife read beautifully the names. But he was very sincere and carefully prepared in his own way. When he spoke, even his nervousness was eloquent. The huge audience was deeply moved.

The stereotype of masculine strength is in need of radical rethinking; a strange word like our text is more and more convincing, the more we listen to Paul and look at his life. Once we have accepted its truth, we can see it everywhere. Really strong people don't brag about their strength; they have nothing to prove. Their strength is seen in tenderness toward their wives and children. When strength is demanded, it is given in quiet joy.

I have always admired the bass sections in Russian choral groups. There seems to be no cultural group to match theirs. Recently I was happily surprised to find that the choirs in the Russian Baptist churches were no different. Every church had its large bass section, seemingly composed of huge, barrel-chested men, venting that deep power with marvelous restraint. Then I noticed something else; they were utterly unashamed to express deep feeling near the end of the service. These big, strong men wiped tears like many others, and cared not who saw them. These same men were standing up against an atheist government, which methodically penalized professed Christian believers. It dawned on me that they were probably able to bear the pressure year after year, precisely because they faced and expressed their feelings in the supportive environment of the family of God.

MOVE 4 (Celebration)

They had the same model of manhood as Paul, and the Son of man also was known to shed a few tears (Luke 19:41 and John 11:35). Jesus loved children and was sensitive to the needs of lepers and outcasts. He broke traditions to be available to a woman with an "unclean" hemorrhage. And with all of this, he clearly established himself as a real man.

The best testimony to his witness of manhood was given by a top sergeant of the Roman army of occupation. A legionnaire with responsibility for one hundred men, he was not only a sagacious civil servant of the empire; he was "bad"! He administered beatings that kept all hundred men in line. And it was his to execute the people who were condemned to die, such as Jesus. He was in charge of the blows and torture given our Lord. This rough Roman watched with peculiar fascination as the lashes fell, the crown of thorns pierced Jesus' brow, the nails were driven in, and the weight of his body fell on the nails when the cross thudded at the bottom of the posthole. He had never seen a man take such cruelty with no bitterness and no cry for pity. He held it as long as he could, and then he cried out his admiration: "Truly! truly! this was the Son of God!" (Matt. 27:54 and Mark 15:39). He had never seen such a man, and he didn't care what it cost him to say it. This was a *man!*

It's good to lift weights and jog and keep one's health, but when I survey the wondrous cross on which the Prince of glory died, my heart cries out for *that* kind of manhood. Therefore will I be comfortable with infirmities, reproaches, necessities, persecutions, and distresses, for when I am Jesus' kind of weak, that's when I am truly a man of strength. Amen.

WORKSHEETS FOR SERMON PREPARATION

The first worksheet presented below may be useful in establishing the disciplines for preparing sermons like the above, with moves from within the text and its context. The second applies to narratives, sketches, and studies.

SERMON WITH MOVES FROM TEXT

Sermon Text:
Scripture Lesson (read in worship):
Sermon Title:
Behavioral Purpose:

Use working notes from exegetical study to help determine the following:

Introduction

Move 1: (Stated simply, in one sentence)
(Establish genre of text for the whole sermon, or genre for the first move)
Move 2: (Use a phase of the genre established [a figure, for example], or use a new genre to elaborate the move)
Move 3: (Same as move 2. If this is the final move, it includes the celebration)
Move 4: (If needed)

Check/Evaluate:

1) Does the purpose match the text?
2) Does the introduction raise the issue of purpose?
3) Does the introduction get hearers on board?
4) Does the introduction telegraph the punch?
5) Do moves flow from the text?
6) Do moves flow easily in consciousness?
7) Are moves reasonably balanced?
8) Does celebration relate to the purpose?
9) Is celebration truly celebrative and not admonition?
10) Is celebration as long as the other moves?

NARRATIVE-TYPE SERMON

Sermon Text:
Scripture Lesson (read in worship):
Sermon Title:
Behavioral Purpose:

Introduction (optional with stories):

Setting:
Protagonist/Chief Character:
Conflict/Issue/Complication:
Resolution of Conflict:
Celebration of Resolution:
Crucial and Interesting Details:

Act/Move 1: (Summarize action, in one sentence)
Act/Move 2: (Same)
Act/Move 3: (Same, and if last, includes celebration)
Act/Move 4: (If needed)

Check/Evaluate:

1) Does the purpose match the text?
2) Does the protagonist embody the purpose and attract identification?
3) Does conflict embody the purpose?
4) Does resolution affirm the purpose?
5) Does celebration focus on the purpose?
6) Is suspense or tension properly timed?
7) Is the narrator's perspective consistent?
8) Is the narrator's mode "eyewitness"?

PART II

THE GENRES OF PREACHING

CHAPTER 5

GENRES: GENERAL GUIDELINES

The vehicles used to make the Scriptures come alive perform a great service; yet they seldom get any recognition. For instance, even when preachers use stories or sketches quite effectively, most do so by intuition, having no name for the process. They wouldn't know where to start to teach someone else how to match that effectiveness. In fact, all too often we attribute skills such as verbal picture-painting and captivating figures to native genius. "Some folks have it; some don't." We blame God for not bestowing this kind of talent on us. But the day for that excuse is over, now that we have theories and guidelines that deal with the intuitive and the emotive. We know *why* people are reached in depth. And we know *how* to help anyone reach them who has the basic intelligence God gives with a call to preach, and the voice to hold a decent conversation. All we have to do is recognize the vehicles of experiential encounter and ask the Holy Spirit to help us use them well.

We call these vehicles genres, and each one has a name, as we enumerated in chapter 2. Names help us differentiate types and give each due credit. Of course, we often find that a given piece of effective communication may have aspects that fit several different genres, but this is no problem. As we have said, the issue is effective flow and not choice of nomenclature. Give credit to as many genres as you like.

No matter how we differentiate the genres, they will still hold a great many characteristics in common. So, although a separate chapter treats each of the principal genres, we must first spell out here the rules that apply to all or most of them, such as concrete images, familiar language, familiar details, and timing of impact or emotional involvement.

CONCRETE IMAGES

All the genres treated except the stream of consciousness involve some form of concrete image. An abstract idea comes to life in a concrete entity. People see it in the mind's eye and associate it with a particular truth. So Jesus' parables were all exercises in likening something people could *not* see to something they *could* see and recall for mental reruns. A Samaritan is far more effective in portraying the ideal than a word like *compassion*. Even when an abstract symbol-word gains great power, such as "Freedom" in the sixties, it is because its meaning is grounded in experiences of the concrete denial of that very freedom.

General statements tend to tempt preachers, because religion is full of abstract ideals, and because it is so much easier to speak generally than to use the specific, often agrarian images so common in both Old and New Testaments. It is easier to sound wise and grandiose with the sweeping implications of generality. But without the pictures, the people don't use the abstract ideal; it often fails to form at all in consciousness.

So the setting for every narrative is a *specific place*, at a *specific time*, and an act is performed by a *specific person*. The preacher does not say, "We often do or say. . . ." Specifying can be overdone, of course, but the minimum of concretes must be there if the picture or setting is to form in the mind's eye. The hay in the manger in the sermon in chapter 9 is crucial to *seeing* the Nativity. The hay is what enables the hearer to grasp more fully the final meaning of the whole sermon.

Rather than cheapen or lower the message, concretes generate the deep respect and gratitude born of nourishment. Concretes are earthy details with heavenly impact, because they draw people into identification and self-recognition in a way utterly impossible with broad generalities. After the picture is clear, and when it is time to celebrate, *then* one can lead the congregation in authentic, celebrative generalities. That is where they function well.

FAMILIAR LANGUAGE

Genres couched in familiar language help hearers identify with and enter into growth encounters. One of the most effective ways to block the formation of concepts in consciousness is to speak in unfamiliar language. It is seen as putting on airs and establishing a social distance from the hearers. Some of this involves "big words," which ordinary people neither use nor understand. At other times the problem is simply that the words are alien: English and simple, but not *"our"* simple English. The people hear the word as alien, and relate to the speaker in the same way. People identify with speakers whose identity with the audience is signaled by their use of the language and images familiar to the audience.

This insight is evident in the way some people relate to youth. No matter how old the speaker is, the use of the latest youth lingo will procure her or him a bond with the teenagers. No matter how young the speaker is, the use of what seems to be stilted and strange lingo will result in inattention or being tuned out, for being perceived as ''out of touch.'' Familiar language is a way of saying that the speaker identifies with the hearers, whatever the genre being used.

Identification with the speaker is important, because this rapport helps to generate identification with the story or other genre being used by the speaker. The eyewitness mode enhances the effectiveness of the vehicles. And the audience which bonds with the eyewitness preacher is that much closer to and involved with the action in the tale told. The folktales of earlier cultures were effective precisely because familiar idiom facilitated closer bonds between tellers and hearers. This brought vastly better understanding, and planted the social contract of the ''primitive society'' in a functional and sophisticated way. Language helps the teller to be a ''significant other.''

FAMILIAR DETAILS

Just as familiar language begets a bond with the hearers and a better grasp of and obedience to the message, so also do the familiar details in the genre. Clarence Jordan's version of the parables of Jesus is so very effective for his southwest Georgia hearers just because the rich man in the story serves mint juleps and collard greens. The hearers see it the minute he frames it in these terms. Sandy Ray helps us into Jesus' parable of the builder who had to count the cost ahead of time. He is looking at it in his mind's eye, but now he is looking ahead at the number of electrical outlets on a given wall. The basic purpose of Jesus is more than fulfilled with this clear and common detail from the building trade.

As I write these very words, it occurs to me that these examples have come from memory. There was no need to look up a reference; the image formed in my memory many years ago, and it won't go away. A preacher talked of the crucifixion of Jesus at a youth camp vesper more than forty years ago. And I can still tell the story, because he mentioned concrete and familiar details like the hobnail boots of the centurion and his soldiers. I heard the cross thump when it hit the bottom of the posthole, and I saw the flesh tear, when the weight of Christ's body suddenly hung from those huge nails. In answer to the question of the spiritual "Were You There?" I must say "Yes." That preacher took me there with the visualization of the scene on Calvary.

ON TIMING OF IMPACT

Finally, all of the genres—indeed, all other means of good homiletic communication—require careful timing of emotional involvement and suspense. The timing for suspense is easy enough to visualize. The tale-teller is warned against revealing the resolution of the conflict too soon, since this suspense is the "hook" that keeps the listener vicariously involved. A premature resolution renders the rest of the tale anticlimactic and uninteresting. This suggests a purposeful escalation of tension and suspense right up to the resolution. This is accomplished by the carefully timed release of the facts and action of any of the genres, leading up to the solution, resolution, or other conclusion. The celebration follows immediately.

This kind of self-restraint is easy to understand but hard to implement. All too many introductions "telegraph the punch" of the whole sermon and thus take away all possible suspense. The way in which Christ is the answer, for instance, is trumpeted in the first paragraph, if not the first sentence. One has nothing to anticipate. On the other hand, this does not mean that we hide the text to keep our intent a secret. It simply means that we offer the text in such a way that there is still something to be sought to make the experience of the text complete.

The timing of involvement is more complicated, although very close to the timing of suspense in the various forms of sequential or narrative material. The material in all of the genres must be sequenced in such a way that the hearer's involvement increases, rather than decreases. On an imaginary Richter scale for the purpose, the preacher estimates the emotional impact of the various elements in a sermon, and arranges them so that they increase rather than decline.

On occasion, this poses problems. A classic illustration of the timing dilemma is encountered in the action sequence in the Parable of the Last Judgment (Matt. 25:34-46). The problem faced here is how to end with high celebration, when the sequence of moves in the story ends with the bad news of the condemned. Especially in a sermon-length exposition, one simply must not try to celebrate or be glad about human loss. Several answers have been devised, none of which is fully satisfactory. Here are two possibilities:

1) The narrator tells the second part first and then tells the part about the blessed, moving from that into celebration (arbitrarily reversing the original sequence).
2) The narrator tells the story in a low key and in sequence, respecting the original flow, and returns to retell the conclusion of the first part in the celebrative mode.

In my earlier work *The Recovery of Preaching*, I have commented at length about the sequencing of whole moves for ascending impact. In the flow of a sermon as first conceived, the preacher may assume that the rule of logical sequence is at odds with the rule of emotional flow. The typical professional then yields to the abstract logic rather than the emotional logic. Of course, the encounter is destroyed. The point is that there is a variety of logical possibilities, not just one deductive mode.

It is also true that people's emotions have a logic of their own, which demands movement up. Without consciously deciding to do so, they turn off that which has turned downward. We call it anticlimax. Because of this, great art, whether symphony, drama, or sermon, moves to the climax and then subsides. One dare not violate this logic.

The ideal answer is to find a way to merge the two logics. One can experiment with different kinds of abstract logic. 9, 7, 5, 3, 1 is as logical as 1, 3, 5, 7, 9. One then chooses between the logical sequences on the basis of the logic of the emotions.

The appropriateness of this kind of planning for the purposes of worship is well established. Western culture has long accepted poetry, drama, and cantatas, which end with celebrative qualities. All of these not only tolerate freely expressive ends but they also *require* a moving last stanza, symphonic movement, or final act. As is true of the sermon, it is important in these fine art forms also that emotional logic prevail. It is this intuitive logic that causes audiences to grow restless when the rules of escalating suspense and emotional impact are violated. As we have said, the artist and the theologian must never be in conflict, but each can and must maintain a creative and functional integrity.

Authentic celebration, then, depends on this upward movement, this mounting emotional involvement of the congregation. Whether there is a story plot with a gripping conflict, a deeply moving illustration, or some other set of entities generating great identification, all must be evaluated by the sermon writer on the intuitive emotional Richter scale. The genre employed must make rational sense, but the sequence must also make emotional sense.

This principle of increasing impact is illustrated in chapter 7 (p. 104), in the sermon "Thanks in *Every*thing?" The moves are as follows:

Introduction   This is Thanksgiving, and Paul says thank God in everything.
Move 1   Paul himself is thankful no matter what.
Move 2   There are times when he actually tells us why.
Move 3   His thanks are based on a Providence we often do not see.
Move 4   Seeing Paul's faith and looking back at my own life, I can give thanks the same way from now on.

A similar movement upward is seen in the sermon "A New Model for Macho," found above in chapter 4 (p. 71):

Introduction   Most men brag of their manhood, but the text says the reverse.
Move 1   Paul is stronger when he faces his physical weakness.
Move 2   Paul is stronger when he faces his mental limitations.
Move 3   Paul is stronger facing his spiritual-emotional limitations.
Move 4   The strength comes from the most manly model of all, Jesus.

In both of these examples, the sermon's main genre is a personality sketch, in which the sub-sketches have been arranged according to the writer's discretion. In both, the moves have increasing impact, as they are elaborated with brief narratives or shorter sketches. Although these summary sentences do not give any clue to the move's real weight, this escalating impact is calculated on the basis of the effectiveness of the vehicle or vehicles used to provide each move with an experiential encounter.

I often judge weight on the basis of how a given story or other illustration strikes me. If it moves me, it at least guarantees that when the time comes to lead the celebration, I will engage in authentic gladness. This raises questions in class when a student suspects that there will be Sundays when celebration is impossible in the preacher's soul. Two responses come to mind. One is that the preacher's devotional discipline should guarantee that this happens very seldom. The other is that honesty with officers or even the whole congregation may move them to undergird the preacher enough to enable him or her to overcome the depression. Or, the congregation may just take responsibility for the celebrating.

In the minds of some, this plotting of an upward movement raises even deeper questions about integrity. Frequently, persons unfamiliar with deeply moving communication have accused this timing concern of being a form of manipulation. It is all too easy to use it just as charged, but we must not throw out the baby with the bath water. The authentic pulpit artist is under strict obligation to be, at the same time, an authentic expositor of the Bible and priest of the church of God. That pulpit artist is worthy of greater approval when his or her finale brings the congregation to the worship equivalent of a standing ovation for a great symphonic rendition. The chief difference is that the praise goes primarily to God rather than the preacher.

The timing of emotional impact, then, is a laudable and essential concern without which saving, healing, and empowering influence on the total person would be less likely, if not indeed impossible. It must be engaged in with discipline and integrity, never apologetically, and, it is hoped, with less and less cultural inhibition and more and more openness to the spontaneity of the Holy Spirit. The effort necessary to learn the subtleties of the timing of impact will never be regretted. The pain of starting over, where necessary, will be rewarded beyond your fondest expectations, and God will probably use you as you have never been used before.

With these guidelines to govern the content and style of all the genres, we turn now to a discussion of the genres themselves.

CHAPTER 6

THE NARRATIVE

My foot standeth in an even place:
in the congregations will I bless the Lord.
That I may publish with the voice of thanksgiving,
and tell *of all thy wondrous works.*

(Ps. 26:12, 7)

The first and most important of the genres or vehicles of encounter is the narrative. It is the one most common in folk culture and can be said to be the easiest to use. The tale well told is a marvelous means for reaching the whole of a person, appealing to the intellect, providing vicarious experiences for the feeding of the intuitive tapes of faith, and setting the fires of emotional joy which culminate in celebration.

What scholars formally refer to as salvation history may also be thought of as an extended *tale* about the workings of God in human experience. Indeed, this history was originally preserved as a kind of folk narrative, to be told in praise and celebration, with nurture thrown in for good measure. It was not a corpus of material to be scientifically analyzed. It could even be argued that the Incarnation is described best as God's effort to reconcile humanity by way of a lived out *story,* seen and heard and felt. The theories or doctrines about God seem not to communicate as well as a simple human drama. The Word still reaches us best as story, picture, and song.

Therefore, what some people call "narrative theology" and what others call simply "telling the story" is not an exotic option or primitive novelty, to be chosen and used at the preacher's whim. Nor may one claim that only a born storyteller can succeed with narrative. As I suggested in the preceding chapter, there are ways for any preacher to learn storytelling. Either one tells the gospel story and makes it live, or one's preaching power is greatly limited for changing lives. All the various genres presented here perform the same general function of making the Bible account into a living experience. From and for such experiences the Bible was originally written.

Of course, the term *narrative theology* rightly suggests that the function of stories is not limited to the experiential. Yet it is far more effective to say that "the Kingdom is *like*" this or that parable or Bible character than to say that it *is* this or that abstract term, no matter how well the term is understood. All of us need to engage in orderly thought about God, or theology, as a guide and as a check for coherence. The point is simply that stories, pictures, and other symbolic representations are more understandable and actually more *accurate*. This "gut" faith cannot even be thought about until one has it. The place of doctrine as abstract statement, or even as narrative theology, is subordinate and subsequent to the gospel affirmations as they are personally encountered and embraced through the vehicles of *experience*.

It sounds reasonable enough to say that the narrative is the best vehicle of experience, but there are influential scholars of the art of homiletics who have reservations about stories. This means only that there is need for clarity on exactly what is meant. How does one distinguish between the stories rightfully opposed and the stories herein?

The stories offered here are never simply "warm-ups" or clever attention-getters; they are either drawn from the Bible or used in the direct service of the gospel. They must also be somehow entertaining, since the opposite of entertaining is not educational but boring. They must have a proper sequence and enough suspense to command and reward rapt attention. The stories scholars oppose, however, tend to be irrelevant to the gospel and used more to attract attention to the speaker than to the Word of God.

To serve the Word, stories must motivate a deep and meaningful identification with the Bible action, which, in turn, will generate a vicarious experience of truth. This is what justifies the tale and its enjoyment. Opened are the portals of deep consciousness to the very gospel itself, which is written on the fleshy tablets of the heart, or recorded, with the aid of the Holy Spirit, in the intuitive tapes of the hearer.

This raises the issue of behaviorist psychology. More than one student has offered a suspicion that figurative terms such as the "recording over of intuitive tapes" suggest mechanisms overriding free will. This issue is of great magnitude and is treated at length in chapter 12. Suffice it here to cite Paul's wisdom, to the effect that we only plant and water. *If* there is any increase, it will always be God who brings that salvation and growth.

God gives life to the seed of faith in the soul of the hearer, but the preacher must give life to the story. There are many ways to describe this technically, and we will discuss these later. It may be good first, however, to restate the fact that personal testimony is, in some respects, the best model known for the narrative. This stems first of all from the fact that the teller of a personal testimony-narrative was an *eye-witness* of the event described. In my book *Black Preaching*, I insisted that *all* narratives from the Bible ought to be told as if one had seen them. It makes no sense to expect the hearer to see the manger or the cross if the one who is preaching hasn't seen it. Recent Bible scholars rightly suggest that laity and clergy alike read the Bible in the mode of being present in the stories read, rather than comb the material for ideas. This is old hat in Black tradition, in which it is common to hear a preacher declare that he or she saw John on the Isle of Patmos, early one Sunday morning. The preacher did in fact visualize John and could make the audience see him also. The personal testimony is a good example of narration simply because the teller actually saw and was deeply involved in the story of her or his own experience of salvation. It is just such involvement which must give life to all narratives in preaching.

This deep involvement adds to the effectiveness of the visualization so essential to eyewitness accounts. One "saw" it, not as a detached bystander, but as a deeply concerned person—almost as a relative or a close friend. The technical term is "participant-observer." One reads about David or Paul so long and with such interest that eventually it is as if one grew up on the same block with him. It takes scholarship, in most cases, to dig up the tiny details that enable Bible characters to come alive, but it takes involvement of the teller to bring those research results to the point of living representation. We often wonder why a not particularly well-trained preacher brings to light some fresh insight from the Bible, and why we didn't see it when we read the same passage. The answer lies in the way the preacher has joined in with the action and come up with authentic visions of the story as an eyewitness.

Thus, the personal testimony must have about it a clarity and vividness that enables the hearer readily to identify with the story or to "come aboard." The preacher is painting word pictures out of personally familiar experience, so that the span of years since the tale happened historically is not important. The picture or setting and the actions of the characters are easily and gladly grasped. It is a matter of clear vision on the part of the speaker, and vivid and enthusiastic recounting to a now-involved hearer.

The final parallel between the testimony and all other narratives is that when it is told, it calls forth response because it deals with that which is familiar and deeply meaningful to all. A congregation of hearers who have had similar experiences of salvation quickly *identifies* with the personal details of the narrative. The story takes on a life of its own within the hearer, in much the manner of a television rerun. Old African "Praying Grounds," modern church architecture, shrines, and holy places are all designed to do the same thing: call forth remembrance of the times when one was, as Wesley termed it, "strangely warmed." The Lord's Supper itself is Jesus' way of guaranteeing that we will not lose personal identification with and into the narrative of the crucifixion.

This powerful identification need not be limited to stories of personal conversions, or Jesus' crucifixion. I have seen decisive identifications take place on the basis of such seemingly minor events as a sandwich eaten years earlier in a parsonage. One fifty-year-old male accepted salvation on the basis of a striking correlation between something the preacher said and something from a letter he had just received from his mother. The whole congregation was vicariously blessed by being witness to an authentic adult conversion: a big, strong man with tears streaming down his face, surprised by the Holy Spirit, pulling from his shirt pocket a fresh letter from his mother. This will always remain in their own pools of holy moments for recall and personal identification. It is one of the best-kept secrets of homiletics that our lives are full of holy places and experiences. Persons are best helped to grow and mature, not by negative criticism and supposedly prophetic reproof and admonition, but by the recall of and identification with their own best encounters with God, often in the least likely places.

So, what does one do to be used of God to generate self-recognitions and identifications which become experiences of the gospel and of the presence of God? That is, what does one do besides studying the Word in the mode of being present in it as one reads? And what besides prayer and meditation? Perhaps the best place to begin is with narrative focus.

NARRATIVE FOCUS

Vivid description, employing well-chosen adjectives and compelling the involvement of the hearer, is useless without focus. This is the discipline whereby one determines the aim of the impact. The extent of the impact is in the hands of God, but the aim is at least in part in the hands of the preacher-narrator.

Every good story or drama has a setting, a protagonist, a conflict, and a resolution; for preaching purposes the only difference is the addition of a *celebration* of the resolution. Focus is a matter of unifying all these elements so that they aim at the same goal. To do this, one has first to determine the goal of this good story, the controlling idea or *behavioral purpose* (described in ch. 3). It is this purpose, in combination with the scriptural text, around which the story is focused (cf. the sample worksheet at the end of ch. 4).

Jesus told the Parable of the Good Samaritan to move people to compassion for the suffering, with a possible secondary purpose of changing attitudes toward the Samaritan ethnic group, as Luke records it. Jewish literature had many such tales, each for a *purpose*. Thus, to tell Luke's Parable of the Prodigal Son, with the purpose of helping prisoners come to themselves and return to the faith, one needs to set the story up for that purpose.

The son should be described as a "baby brother" whose place in the family was given no real respect, and who had no authority over anything. If the father was away, the older brother was the boss. All the details should be sympathetic to the younger brother, in an obvious effort to tell the tale from his point of view and help the prison audience to identify with him. To describe the younger son in typical judgmental terms would drive the audience away from him, so purpose determines the son's characterization.

Again, the home from which the son fled should also be a very comfortable and attractive place, and the father needs to be set up as the kindest of men. The father just would not arbitrarily override his son's self-styled ambitions and rebellion. To set him up otherwise would make return to him impossible. The eyewitness teller needs to have empathy for the son, but admiration for the father. The choice of behavioral purpose determines this and also determines that the main character is the son and not the father. It is the son with whom we wish the hearer to identify, because it is the son's growth we wish to see duplicated in the lives of the self-recognizing audience.

The choice of conflict comes next; what is the question which maintains the suspense essential to this tale? One is tempted to engage in complicated psychological descriptions, but the real conflict is always best stated in disarmingly simple terms: Will the boy go home? If the purpose were something else, like encouraging fathers to forgive, the conflict would be, Will the father welcome him home and forgive? This statement of conflict determines the main movement of the story. It is formed by asking if the sermon's behavioral purpose will be achieved in the main character. The story can be described as the orderly movement toward the answer to this uncomplicated question, "orderly" meaning sequential, with increasing build-up of suspense.

With so simple a conflict, the resolution can be even simpler: yes or no. The details of how and when and why may be brilliantly dramatized, but the resolution must be basically no more than a yes or no to the question, Will the boy go home? At the point where this question is answered, the story is essentially finished. Anything more than a brief winding down will be anticlimactic. When the conflict is over and the plot worked out, the story is now completed.

Usually, the presentation of a story ends when the conflict is resolved, but not so with the gospel sermon. In chapter 4 we saw the need for a celebration. And just as the protagonist, conflict, and resolution must deal with the issue embodied in the purpose, so must the celebration. This is the time when the involved preacher and audience express gladness over the resolution of the conflict.

Right away, there may be a question about this being anticlimactic. The answer is that anything other than a celebration would be just that. If the tale is followed by celebration, however, the movement is still upward, and the purpose is still being fulfilled. There is gladness, which amounts to a kind of final blow or ecstatic reinforcement of the lesson. People *remember* what they get glad about, and they have not only intellectual recall but also changed response and spiritual growth. There are bounds beyond which the ecstasy of celebration ought not to go, but there are also levels of ecstasy in every culture beneath which the cognitive recall *and* the affective life-change are both forfeited.

The prodigal son was guest of honor at a dinner or feast, and he was no doubt extremely happy about it. The purpose of the celebration is to help the hearer join the feast and be influenced with the same emotions of joy about having gone "home" to the loving faith once misread as crushing, overly dominant authority. One has not stopped teaching just because one has ceased to present new ideas. Celebration confirms the lesson already taught, etching it deeply on the fleshy tablets of the human heart.

Focus is a hard but helpful discipline. One knows why the description is important and exactly what it is supposed to accomplish. One knows where the story is going, and when it is over. Yet, the story is told quite informally, maintaining its powerful focus in the manner of a folktale teller assuming the stance of an eyewitness, not a research scholar. From early Old Testament times to now, stories have been told for a purpose, and we return to the discipline of narrative focus more as intellectual prodigals than as creative innovators.

VISUALIZATION

Sharing equal importance with narrative focus is inner visual focus, or the empowerment of the hearer to visualize the scene and the action of the story. It is this process of picture-painting and dramatic description which unmistakably moves the hearing experience from thinly veiled cognitive recall to involvement of the total hearer in a meaningful vicarious experience. The identity and self-recognition of which so much has been said, are born of visualization—having seen, for instance, the prodigal son and subsequently having seen how much he resembles "me."

Visualization so intensive requires descriptive details. One can give too many and lose focus, since each detail is a symbolic suggestion of direction or emphasis. Or one can give too few details, causing the image to die aborning, failing to form for lack of concreteness. In between is enough description to tell all of what needs to be known for a hearer to see the picture and come aboard for the purpose chosen.

To find these details one has to use a great deal of ingenuity, both in exegetical study and in imaginative projection beyond the hard data, but in harmony with that which is known. Here, again, are possible extremes. One can go too far and become so detailed as to destroy credibility among thinking people, even granted that they accept preaching as art, not argument. On the other hand, one can be so sparse and vague as to raise questions about one's thoroughness of preparation or the value of even speaking of something of which so little is known.

Not long ago I heard Caesar A. W. Clark preaching about Goliath. This story has always been a favorite, and I recalled particularly the

Bible story story-telling contests of my junior high school days in the YMCA. The two stories most told were "David and Goliath" and "Samson and Delilah," the former holding the lead. But we boys never commanded attention like this Bible story raconteur, Dr. Clark. It dawned on me that he was so gripping because his own vision of the giant was so graphic and clear, setting forth the awesome dimensions of the man Goliath with easily grasped biblical specifics. Making no apparent attempt at effect, indeed almost as if to downplay these statistics, he calmly listed the height of the man at thirteen feet, four inches. Goliath's spear, he said, weighed only twenty-three-and-a-half pounds, and his coat of mail weighed a hundred-ninety-four-and-a-half pounds. Then came his description of the helmet of quilted linen and metal scales, the targets of brass on the breastplate, and so on. The effect on the audience was almost hypnotic, for they were busy looking at Goliath. It does not matter that some scholars think Goliath's height was closer to ten or eleven feet, with other details also scaled down. The point is that this was an awesomely huge and well-armed man, and that this *child*, David, to all intents and purposes, challenged him in the name of the living God. And *we* saw it!

The story went on, the audience all solidly aboard. Everybody knew how the story ended, but everybody was eagerly awaiting how *this* teller would bring it out. Between curiosity about the rendition and a kind of identification inside the story, the suspense was almost unbearable. The story and side comments just kept building, until we reached the ultimate goal of the celebration, which, after such involvement in the story, was quite authentic.

THE USES OF THE NARRATIVE

As we have already seen in chapter 2, there are more uses for narratives than the one-story sermon. Most Bible records contain less than enough material, no matter how reconstituted, to sustain a twenty-minute homily. The one-story sermon which follows is a rarity in most preachers' experience, being more a model of narration as such than a pattern for the majority of a given preacher's weekly offerings of the Word. What, then, are the other options?

Every move in every sermon has to have some means of making its message come alive and engage the hearer. Almost never can the cleverness of word or the power of voice be depended on entirely to provide a deep experiential encounter. As we have seen, this is where the genres come in, and chief among these is the narrative. In this role, the story may be one of several stories, each used in a different homiletic move. Or there may be a story at this move, a picture at another, and a stream of consciousness at still another. The chief concern is that the story serve the purposes of the sermon, and that its length be proportionate to its importance in the sermon. And, of course, the best story is always saved for last, in the celebration.

There is a sense in which every case history, personality sketch, and what have you is a collection of brief narratives. To be arbitrary about assigning a hard and fast designation of genre to an element in a move is fruitless and even counterproductive. The chief concern is not about naming the genre, but about making the Word become vivid and alive.

The brief story-base or short narrative sequence may be used as a framework for a greatly expanded treatment. The main part of the sermon in this case is composed of what may be referred to as "asides" or side comments on the flow of the narrative. These are relevant and often clever parallels from everyday life, focusing, it is hoped, on one behavioral purpose. One decides according to the character of the biblical material and the way one feels led, whether or not to treat the story alone or to emphasize modern parallels.

One final word has to do with the use of stories in the introduction. To tell a story complete with resolution is likely to telegraph the point. The best wisdom here would seem to be that if a story is used in the introduction, only enough of it to raise the issue should be employed. One would then give the answer to the suspense raised at the appropriate place, near the end of the sermon. A whole story may be a whole sermon, or at least a whole insight, whereas a sermonic introduction has only the task of raising the need for those insights. The story then must raise the question without answering it.

Generally speaking, it must be understood that the story has been the chief vehicle of perhaps all the world's civilizations, as they have sought to induct the young into the society, and to impress them with the social contract. When societies have "advanced" beyond the simple tale as educational tool they have almost invariably begun to lose ground in indoctrinating persons for life. Thus, the sterile, didactic teaching which has replaced the story is far from an improvement on Jesus' method. And one of the most helpful means of reviving both pulpit and classroom would be a disciplined and actually very sophisticated return to the use of stories and symbolic myth.

A SAMPLE NARRATIVE SERMON

In some respects, the best-told story in the Bible is the least respected by scholars. The book of Esther does not mention God. Its historicity is seriously questioned. In the minds of many, it is full of fierce nationalism. Yet its action is fast and compelling, and there are interpretations of its message well worth hearing and heeding. What is offered here, then, is a treatment of this story, given as story, in a manner that translates it into modern language and issues. The preacher is Ella P. Mitchell, and she has delivered versions of it at such places as the Rankin Chapel, Howard University, and an annual meeting of the Church Women United of Southern California. For each audience there may be a different behavioral purpose in mind. The purpose in this version is that of strengthening the hearers' sense of vocation, or call from God.

A problem with making this a story-sermon exclusively, with no further comment, as can be done with the Parable of the Prodigal Son, lies in the fact that the text and main focus occur somewhere around the middle of the story. There are two choices. (1) One can climax the story at the point where Esther agrees to accept her call and risk her life. One would then use the victory at the end as celebration, risking the theological implications of a bloody rejoicing. (2) One can tell the whole story, which is possibly what the audience would enjoy, and then engage in extended comment on the text. The first approach is far superior from an artistic perspective, since the better form is not normally to tell a story and then explain its application or moral. The second choice, in the sermon that follows, provides an illustration of the folksy tale in today's language. It was chosen for its compelling sense that the teller was an eyewitness, personally identified with the main character, and able to draw her audience to identify likewise.

FOR SUCH A TIME

> And who knoweth whether thou art come to the
> kingdom for such a time as this?
>
> *(Esther 4:14c)*

Introduction

I suppose there is no greater challenge among us than the one we call male chauvinism. Tons of material are printed decrying an evil which we [women] as a clear majority of the population are actually supporting. At the heart of all of this, however, is an issue which we overlook and which is applicable to men as well as women, of whatever race or culture. It is the question of what every human being was born to be and to do. In or out of what*ever* identity, why was each of us born? One of my favorite Bible stories may be said to speak to this issue, while addressing some others. It is even now one of the most celebrated stories in the Hebrew tradition.

MOVE 1

The setting is Babylon or Persia, now famous as Iran, where the Jews were taken in exile from the Promised Land. The chief character is Hadassah or Esther, a very beautiful young woman, referred to in scripture as a "maiden." The king is a man named Ahasuerus [Ay-haz-you-air-us], better known to us as Xerxes. He has been classified in Western history as a great emperor, but the Jews were very candid in their supposed recording of his personal habits. He drank too much too often, and was known to do very foolish things when he was inebriated or "stoned."

On one such occasion, when he had tarried too long at the cups, he got to boasting, as the "boys" often do. He was declaring the beauty of his queen in terms too intimate for good taste. In response to one man's playful challenge he even went so far as to order Queen Vashti to dance before his guests in what was to have been both a topless and a bottomless exhibition. She was outraged, of course, and sternly refused to obey his order. This precipitated a major crisis of state.

The king's overreaction stemmed from his fear (and that of his guests) that if the word got out that she had refused his order, *all* the women would break out of their quiet submission and refuse to obey their husbands also. The male courtiers were horrified. The king's counselors advised him that there was nothing to do but to make of Vashti an example of strict punishment. The word was published in every language spoken in the combined kingdoms: "According to the laws of the Medes and the Persians, which change not, this woman Vashti shall never again come before the King, and her place shall be given to another and more worthy person. Let every man bear rule in his own home."

Since this was a permanent demotion, a search was instituted to find her replacement. The announcement was posted far and wide and a Jew named Mordecai read it one afternoon, and made a mental note of it. His mind flashed back to Esther, who had been orphaned and was now entrusted to his fatherly care, even though he was only a cousin, technically speaking. "She is a lovely creature and quite intelligent. She would make a fantastic queen," he thought.

So Mordecai plotted and planned to have her considered among those to be presented as candidates for the office of queen. He was careful not to reveal that this beautiful damsel was a Jewess. For a whole year he worked with her, teaching her the graces of the court and having her treated with all the best lotions and other ancient cosmetics available. She was a good subject, and the hard work and prayer and fasting brought excellent results.

Finally the day came when Esther had her chance, and she performed so well that she made it all the way to the Babylonian throne, still undiscovered as a Jew, and now widely admired and respected.

MOVE 2

Things were looking up for the Jews, that is until the wicked Haman, the king's vizier or chief administrator, encountered Mordecai one day in the marketplace. It seems old Cousin Mordecai didn't feel like bowing before Haman just because he was vizier. Old Haman bristled at what he took to be Mordecai's flagrant disrespect, and it bugged him to no end. He developed an intense hatred for Mordecai and extended it to all the Jewish people.

In his obsessive interest in getting even, he devised a demonic scheme in which the king would declare that all persons belonging to a subversive group not named in the decree would be subject to death by mob violence. That is, any citizen not a member of the group was given power not only to lynch them but also to take possession of their property. The king was to receive a sizable payment from the hand of Haman, also. The date set for the massacre was the thirteenth day of the month of Adar, and the order was made into unchangeable law by the seal of the king's ring.

Meanwhile, when Cousin Mordecai got wind of this cynical and monstrous plot, he put on sackcloth and ashes and paced up and down outside the palace gate. When Esther heard of his antics, she sent a servant out with clothing and supplies. By refusing to accept anything that was offered, he made it quite plain that something was seriously wrong. He sent her a copy of the king's decree and a note requesting that she intercede for her people.

Esther was severely torn and in great jeopardy. Even a queen was not to go before the king unless bidden, and the penalty for an uninvited appearance could go as high as death. Esther reminded Cousin Mordecai of all of this in her note, and he replied that he was the one who taught *her* the law. Of *course* he knew the dangers. However, he insisted, "Think not that you will escape in the king's house, more than all the other Jews. For if you hold your peace at this time, then shall the enlargement and deliverance of the Jews arise from another place; but you and your father's house shall be destroyed: and who knows but what you are come to this kingdom for just such a time as this?"

MOVE 3

Esther's answer was swift and to the point. She asked her surrogate uncle to gather all the Jews and have them to fast and pray for three days. She and her maidens would do likewise. At the end of this spiritual preparation she would go to the king, whatever the risk. She was steeled in her mind by the awareness that she could do no more than die in either case. She said, "If I perish, I perish." It was better to die in an act of courage than to be tracked down and devoured in cowardice.

When the days of preparation were accomplished, Esther adorned herself in one of her finest gowns and broke precedent by taking the initiative and asking to be admitted to the king's inner court. When the king saw her standing in the arched opening at the far end of the chamber, he held out his golden sceptre, indicating that her life was in no danger. Then he said, "What can I do for you? What would you like? Whatever it is, you can have anything up to half of my kingdom."

That was unexpectedly good news, but Esther displayed admirable calm and laudable restraint. She had a game plan that required more time and subtlety to bring the proper results. "O King, if you and your grand vizier, Haman, were to come to a banquet that I will prepare, I would be most pleased." The king's response was so quick it startled Esther. He still wanted to know if she wanted something beyond so simple a petition as attendance at a banquet. *Any*body would grant that, and gladly.

Haman was ecstatic. He had made it to the top, not only with the king but with the queen as well. As he neared his home, he came across Mordecai, his pet peeve. But his feelings mended after he arrived home and gleefully shared with his family the news that "the queen doesn't want anybody at her fine banquet but me and the king!" But he confessed that all this meant very little so long as he still had to see Mordecai hanging around the palace gate. They decided to build a gallows and ask the king to have Mordecai hung the next day. After the execution, he would really be able to enjoy the banquet to the full.

Meanwhile, the king was unusually restless. In the absence of sleeping pills, he ordered some court Minutes to be read. He was *always* so bored with them that he fell asleep. That night it didn't work. He heard something that really caught his attention. "What's this about a Mordecai who uncovered a plot to kill the king? Has any honor been bestowed on him for this important act of loyalty?" The answer was that nobody could remember any such, so the king resolved to correct the matter. When Haman arrived at court to ask for the hanging of Mordecai, the king spoke first. He asked him what should be done to the man whom the king wanted to honor. Good old Haman just knew he was the one, so he dreamed up a real spectacle. "Let the royal apparel be brought which the king used to wear, and the horse he has ridden on, and the crown which he has worn, and let the noble princes dress him and lead him through the streets on horseback. Thus should it be done with the man whom the king delights to honor." Then the king said, "O.K.! That's fine. Make haste and do this for Mordecai the Jew that sits at the king's gate. Let nothing fail of all the plan you have proposed."

MOVE/ACT 4 (Celebration)

Haman went home sick with sadness, with his head covered, and told his folks all about it. They knew he was doomed. Nevertheless, the chamberlain came and escorted Haman to Esther's banquet. After dinner, the king asked, "O Queen Esther, what is your petition, and just as I told you, it will be performed, even to half of my kingdom." Esther summoned all the courage she could muster, and no little diplomacy. "Please let my people be given their lives at my request. We have been decreed to be destroyed, not just enslaved but murdered." The secret was out; Esther was a Jew. What honesty! What dedication to her calling! "I know you can't change a decree once it is sealed and issued. But I just had to *ask* you to save us anyway.''

The king's quick response was, ''Who on earth dared to cook up such a cruel policy? Where is he who dares to presume in his heart to do such a dastardly thing?'' Esther pointed to Haman. The king arose angrily and paced back and forth in the palace garden, just outside the door. Meanwhile, Haman pled for his life to Esther, the queen. When the king came back, he saw the strange spectacle of Haman on the side of Esther's couch, pleading. He roared, ''You mean this rascal has the nerve to try for my wife, also?'' He was caught up by the guards and his head covered. He was hanged that same day on the gallows he had prepared for Mordecai. It was a terrible scene, but the Jews were safe, and the queen had risen to the full stature of the person she was called to be.

Yes, God was not mentioned, but everybody knew that God had called Esther from the very beginning. It was God who had given her great talent and beauty. Jehovah, Lord of all, had made all the arrangements for a deliverance of which Mordecai was certain all along. It was indeed God's plan that Esther be in the Kingdom for just such a time!

What was true of Esther is true of every soul on the face of the earth. Whatever we have and are is part of a calling. Our talents are to be risked in the places to which we are assigned, rather than relished for our own enjoyment. If we perish or triumph, prosper or go bankrupt, we are all in the Kingdom for *this* time, and there is no better way to live or die than in the will of God for our lives. Amen.

CHAPTER 7

THE CHARACTER SKETCH

Our second genre is the character sketch, a combination of biblical data and other materials, designed to bring to full, living proportions a character from the Bible. Other religiously significant persons may also be treated in the same detail, for a homiletic move, or perhaps even for a whole sermon. The person chosen is representative of a trait worthy of emulation, and the hearer so identifies with the person as to become desirous of embodying that trait also. This is a very handy and workable way to build a sermon with focus, and its selection of smaller narratives, illustrative of the trait, is easy to assemble, deliver, and celebrate.

The character sketch is ideal when the text and controlling idea involve an abstract or general statement, set in a scriptural context which has no narrative possibilities at all. One chooses a Bible character who embodies the principle in the text, and then makes a sermon of small sketches of episodes in which the character chosen exemplifies the way one acts when one believes the text.

A good example of the character sketch would be a sermon on I Thessalonians 5:18, on giving thanks in everything. This text occurs amidst a series of admonitions such as ''Rejoice evermore,'' ''Pray without ceasing,'' and ''Quench not the Spirit.'' There is very little of the Thessalonian church's history that would have any exegetical influence on the understanding of the text. The surrounding verses contain nothing that would facilitate the interpretation, since these are things Paul says to ''everybody'' he writes to, so to speak. However, this sweeping, startling exhortation to give thanks is not without a context for comprehension and identification. Paul as *person* speaks out of his own life-style, just as he reminded the folk in his second letter to Corinth that *they* were living epistles to be *read* (3:2). So even if Paul does say this to ''everybody,'' it is from his very gut, a part of the core belief system which ''makes *him* tick.'' If the text sounds a bit extreme, test it out in Paul's own pattern of life, and see if he practices what he preaches, and to what effect.

What can be said of Paul's word on thanks can be said of the other rules he urged people to follow. And what can be said of Paul's ideas can be said of the words attributed to David, or Abraham. Furthermore, even if a given Bible character left no words to sum up her or his beliefs and admonitions, that person was still inescapably a living epistle, and can therefore be used as living proof that a particular principle can be lived out and is worth seeking in real life.

The key to effective character sketches, like that to narration, is study in the mode of presence, rather than the mode of analysis and idea-hunting. The ideas will flood in when one has *experienced* a visit with Paul or David. One reads biblical and other materials with a constant eye for visualization of the character, moving from portrait to active character. The pieces are put together bit by bit, and after a while, the character is a reality in the reader's own religious experience.

This process rises to supreme heights when applied to Jesus Christ. Hymnals contain many songs that talk about such things as coming to the garden alone, but this has too often been reserved for the musical aspect of the liturgy. It is *not* sacrilegious to visualize the Nazarene; but it is a sin for the preacher to study too little and offer an inadequate portrait. The preacher who hasn't fully visualized Jesus will never help the hearers see him. And the picture painted in the pulpit must relate to the audience, just as Sallman related his ''Head of Christ'' to his particular identity group. The point is that a careful and prayerful sketch of a character is not just one of those things a preacher does in desperation, in an effort to be an effective communicator of the gospel. People *need* characters sketched with whom to identify in their vicarious sojourns in the biblical world, even as they also need familiar and beloved models of Christian behavior.

This need for a mental family album of biblical characters is so great as to justify whole sequences of character studies in the regular menu of congregational Bible study. The goal in a sermon, however, is not to cover the biography completely, but to make the *text* come alive. Like all other sermons, the sermon built on a character sketch will be controlled best by a theme and purpose. This is for the sake of artistic integrity and focus, as well as the goals of Christian growth.

In fact, the themes and purposes are what make the characters meaningful. No Christian needs a mental scrapbook of biblical personalities for its own sake. There is no salvation in the ability to show off one's knowledge of the people of Jesus' world. The value of these characters is that each of them brings to living representation some portion of the Word. Just as Jesus can declare that whoever has seen him has seen God (John 14:9), every hero and heroine of the Bible is an embodiment of some aspect of the Word of truth. It is this Word which makes them both interesting and helpful.

Another aspect of helpfulness is these characters' potential for what we have called identification. The danger is that without carefully planning the cast which is to become part of the gospel message, one may provide self-recognition for only a fraction of the congregation. In one study to determine which biblical characters were known to the adults in a community, the only women familiar to the group were the ones after whom their missionary circles were named, and Mary, the mother of Jesus. Just as a collection of well-remembered scriptural texts should be the goal of every preaching pastor and church-school teacher, so also should there be built up in the minds and lives of the hearers a cast of vital, interesting heroes *and heroines* from the Bible for purposes of identification. It ought to happen that members would casually and frequently say things like, ''I feel as Moses felt when . . .'' or ''Be careful how you give up on us Hannahs.''

It hardly needs to be added that what can be said of these characters can be said of all human beings as living or more often posthumous models for identification. As a pastor I made it my business to figure out what word had been best embodied in the life of a deceased person, and this was used as the text for the eulogy. Or I could speak of a soul from scripture and see the grateful recognition, in the eyes of the bereaved, of the parallel with the deceased. The all-too-frequent tragedy was that some had embodied so little.

In this connection it may be helpful to share the fact that only a few persons seem to leave any impression of having had a favorite verse of scripture. But the lives of those who do have often reflected that biblical theme. Our own late son marched unflinchingly to his grave, reminding his own faltering parents that the family's favorite verse was Romans 8:28. With a twinkle in his eye, he urged us not to give up on the idea that God works for good in *all* things. The Paul in the family album was associated with a text, and the combination strengthened both memory and Christian character.

Character sketches are an indispensable aid to spiritual growth. They provide what patron saints do in some cultures, and ancestral and varied other spirits do in others. They give a concreteness to a person's goals for growth and a personal form of encouragement.

What, then, are the guidelines for a character sketch? The quickest way to answer is to say that the character sketch is not radically different from the narrative. It has a protagonist or main character, who embodies the proposed purpose of the sermon. The timing is always similar, and it builds up to a celebration.

The difference is most evident in the fact that the material is drawn from so many more places in the biblical account. The moves also may not follow a strict chronological sequence, to facilitate proper timing. Instead of the narrative conflict, which moves toward a resolution, the sketch may provide a series of incidents-moves, which build from lower to higher impact. Each incident is an example of the text being lived out. Granted these slight technical differences, the keys to the effectiveness of both narratives and character sketches are the same: the protagonist embodies the purpose, and the rigor of sharp focus is maintained throughout the sermon.

Because of this similarity it is often difficult to differentiate between narrative and sketch. The sermon on Paul which follows is a collection of brief narratives, each constituting a move further illustrating the text. Yet they all add up to a sketch of Paul's personality. Chapter 10 presents a combination of character sketch data and insights, strung together in an imaginative dialogue, and some brief narratives, which are inevitable whenever one recounts happenings of any kind.

THANKS IN *EVERY*THING?

In every thing give thanks:
for this is the will of God in Christ Jesus concerning you.
(I Thess. 5:18)

Introduction

I don't seem to pay much attention to Thessalonians until Thanksgiving, when I need a text for the season. Paul's word is very handy, but this year that text seems for some reason to go to more extremes than usual. The apostle Paul is often heard to say things like this, but this year I get the feeling that he has been very serious about it all along. "Brother Paul, do you mean to say *every*?" And the answer echoes back through the corridors of history; "Yesss! *Every*thing!"

That seems a bit much. It evokes a touch of the same response I give to religious fanatics—some of those people who start every conversation with "Praise God!" or "Thank the Lord!" Paul seems to be a thoughtful and reasonable man, and I am a little surprised that he talks like this. But he keeps on saying things like, "That's what I said, and that's what I meant." He challenges me to look at his record and see if he practiced what he so pointedly preached: to see if, as we say, he put his money where his mouth was.

MOVE 1

It turns out that Paul is thankful no matter how difficult the situation. He writes the Philippians, "I thank my God upon every remembrance of you" (1:3). That's typical of Paul but strange, generally speaking. Don't you know that Philippi is where Paul got thrown in jail for healing that girl who told fortunes? Not only that, but he and his party were stripped and *beaten* before they were incarcerated! I would think Paul would wish to forget a place like that. But even in the solitary confinement of the inner prison, with their feet in the stocks, Paul and his friends were singing and praising God. In other words, even in the midst of the darkness, dampness, and danger of the dungeon, they *thanked* God (Acts 16:22-24).

I can't imagine what they were praising God *for,* unless it was for just being alive. Maybe it was like the slaves who thanked God that their "bed was not their cooling board" and for being "clothed in their right minds." Whatever the basis, Paul didn't stop thanking God under even the worst conditions.

MOVE 2

Occasionally one can hear him stating why. It may be subtle, and it is ingenious, but it is definitely thanks. Acts 26 finds Paul, as it were, in handcuffs and hailed before the court. He is an accused prisoner, and he is informed by the court that he is now permitted to speak for himself. The words that come out are in the tested terminology of the court, as we say. It is legal and polite to begin with the words, "I consider myself happy, O king Agrippa, that I am privileged to answer for myself this day before you concerning all those grave charges which have been made against me by the Jews." It is a noble statement, worthy of a man with Paul's training, but how do you go about making it sound so sincere? Here you are preaching the very gospel of our Lord, and yet treated as a common criminal! Surely there is nothing to be thankful about in this crushing defeat of high idealism.

The answer is in between the lines. Paul is saying that he is happy to be in a jurisdiction which gives each person his or her day in court. He is into the proper recognition of the fact that Rome guarantees him due process. He is also delighted to have the hearing before a man known for his unusual familiarity with the customs and questions at issue. However, this is only the first and literal or surface meaning of this courtly address.

Paul in his heart is thanking God that he has this opportunity to speak to a *king!* Agrippa is wearing two hats. He is a sitting judge, but he is also a king. Some people live all their lives, and never get to speak or preach or testify before a king.

Furthermore, most kings can get bored or tired and simply say, "Away with him!" Or they can "turn it off" and stop listening. But this king is also a judge. His throne is also a bench. So he has to hear Paul out. He is in a sense a captive audience, because he is the guarantor of due process. Paul has a committed ear from this royalty. What a privilege indeed!

So, with the amenities behind him, Paul lets loose with his testimony. He tactfully reminds the judge-king that his faultless manner of life from his youth is well known. He moves on through his adult years of strict observance of the law as a Pharisee. He sees himself accused for believing the promise of God to the fathers. Still framing his case in the tested terms of legalese, yet fashioning it as flowing personal testimony, he goes from the persecution of the saints to his conversion and call. Then he moves in for the kill—the juridical coup. With the king's full and rapt attention, he drives home the punch line: "Wherefore, O king Agrippa, I could not be disobedient to the heavenly vision." It is a great stroke! No wonder he is thanking God under his breath!

MOVE 3

This seems to be his pattern throughout. Whether *we* can see what he sees to be thankful for or not, *he* can see it. Perhaps it's because he believes that God works in *every*thing for good (Rom. 8:28). He is strikingly consistent; there's that *every* again. Thanks for him are not just a habit or a courteous gesture; they are based on a well-thought-out belief system. He has a way of interpreting life in the mode of gratitude.

Listen to the beginning of his letter to the church at Philippi, a few verses after the word about thanking God at his every remembrance of them. He is in jail, and he knows they are worried about him. He says (v. 12ff.), "I want you to understand, brothers and sisters, that what has happened to me here in Rome has actually brought about the advancement of the gospel. I get to give my witness before the palace guards and everybody else around here. And there are folks who were once very wishy-washy, who, having seen how I take this imprisonment, are much bolder in the faith. So you see, regardless of how and why they preach, the gospel is indeed preached, and I'm real glad about that."

I would have a hard time taking unjust imprisonment the way Paul does, but I can surely join him in rejoicing, given this distance in time, and 20/20 hindsight. It dawns on me that Paul writes more of the New Testament than any other single individual, and that this would never have happened without Paul's being under house arrest in Rome. Here sits the greatest theological and practical thinker of the early church, with *time to write* only because he is a prisoner. He is a busy, energetic fellow, and he gets around! But God lets him be placed in the relative comfort of a guarded house of his choice, with visitation rights and mail in and out. There is disgrace, perhaps, in being in custody, or under house arrest. But we are all the richer because he was incarcerated, and because he was not crushed by the blow. He chose rather to *work* during confinement, with his heart, mind, and pen. And we are blessed.

Once, many years ago, I heard of the discovery of relics of very early Christian worship in the northern reaches of Germany. There were speculations about how this might have happened so soon after Christ. I had and I still have a theory about this.

It is said that a man named Paul is a house prisoner in Rome, with a different Roman soldier chained to his wrist every day. This fellow writes a lot, but sometimes he gets writer's cramp, so he has to find something else to do. He's not much for taking naps and such, so he looks around for some way to use the time. He sees this soldier chained to him. Why not give *him* some of the Word of God? He starts to communicate, and some listen eagerly. But if they don't, he jerks the chain and wakes them up. Some of them find his witness to be life-changing, and they seek out his followers in the palace and all over Rome.

These same soldiers who guard Paul get sent all over the Roman Empire. One day one of these fellows is talking to another in Northern Germany. They have been transferred up there to do their time in the hinterlands, as are all of the best troops at one time or another. This soldier happens to mention a person named Jesus, and the other one is startled. "How did *you* find out about *him*?" he asks in astonishment. The answer comes back, "They put me on guard duty one day in the home of a strange little guy named Paul. When he finished his correspondence, or whatever it was he was writing, he turned to me and started talking about this man Jesus. I was fascinated, and I wanted to follow him." There are a lot of people on the post who have had the same experience. The word spreads like wildfire. They set up a place of worship, and that's how the Christian relics turned up so very early so far from Rome.

MOVE 4 (Celebration)

God works in *every*thing for good, so we can *thank* God in everything. The very budget of the Roman Empire, which builds an almost timeless system of roads and aqueducts, can be used for missionary purposes. Those very roads can be used to transport missionaries, and they can be won to service while they are still soldiers in uniform and on salary. The Empire's military budget is God's missionary budget. Hallelujah! I *see* now how Paul stays so thankful.

I had some terrible chest pains in a pulpit once, and all of a sudden the breath coming out of my mouth was too weak to be heard. We were only a block from an early detection heart center, one of three in the nation at the time. They rushed me to it, and they let me smell the pretty oxygen. They monitored my heartbeat for days. I am alive today because of an adequate but not life-threatening warning. It happened in a perfect place at a perfect time, but I didn't seem to hear Paul as I should have. Paul might have said, "While you're watching that monitor you're not supposed to be able to see, try thanking God. This is no exception to the rule, and, besides, thanks will help you heal faster. In *every*thing give thanks!"

Whatever happens from now on, I'm going to thank God. In *every*thing? Yes! *Every*thing! Whether it's raining or the sun is shining, in good times and in bad, whether I'm popular or in oblivion, God is worthy of *all* my praise and thanksgiving. Let everything that hath breath praise the Lord! For as long as we have breath, we have something for which to be thankful.

In *every* thing give thanks:
for this is the will of God in Christ Jesus concerning you.

Amen!

CHAPTER 8

THE GROUP STUDY

The term *group study* here denotes the portrayal of a body of people, with its own traits and problems and actions and causes for celebration. It amounts to a parallel to the character sketch. Whatever can be said of a single personality can, in a sense, be said of a group. Congregants find self-recognition and identification as members of the group, which the preacher observes and studies to learn its characteristic features. The information is used in vivid portrayals, just as is done with the characteristics found in individuals.

The group study is used to help move whole groups. Wherever people act as a group, whether formally or informally, it is probably better to try to inspire them as group, rather than as individuals. This is especially true of self-conscious groups who see themselves as powerless or picked on, or bound by longstanding tradition and loyalty. This genre makes use of defensive or loving group identifications to motivate spiritual growth and service.

Because of these same ties, it may be unwise to subject close-knit groups to severe criticism, since group momentum can intensify both acceptance and rejection of the Word. But then *any* predominantly negative approach, whether to individuals or groups, is ineffective. Indeed, it may even injure those who too easily accept verbal punishment, surrendering healthy self-esteem or group esteem in the bargain. Group studies lift up the positive possibilities and common values of a natural community of persons, primarily in celebration. Then the study harnesses them to develop ever greater spiritual maturity and Kingdom service as a body.

The examples presented in this chapter demonstrate the various ways in which any event involving two or more persons, or even a single person symbolizing a group, can be used to motivate and teach another group. The first sample presented is a passage from a sermon by Miles J. Jones, to a worshiping congregation gathered to honor a colloquium of prospective writers. The purpose of the sermon as a whole addressed the needs of the congregation as members of an ethnic minority; the section presented here appeared only incidentally addressed to the writers honored, while speaking still to the whole group.

The message was based on II Kings 5:1-14, the story of Elisha's healing of the Syrian commander, Naaman. The text used was the first verse:

> Now Naaman, captain of the host of the king of Syria, was a great man with his master, and honourable, because by him the Lord had given deliverance unto Syria: he was also a mighty man in valour, *but he was a leper*.

This sermon, under the title "Naaman's Problem and Ours," yielded great motivation for group self-esteem and achievement. There were also relevant insights and sympathetic motivation for dealing with lepers. The audience quickly succumbed to their common bond of visible characteristics generally perceived as more important than character and competence. The hearers readily identified with this man whose great accomplishments were nullified by the word *but* and the word *leper* which followed. The word *Black* was never even mentioned until very near the end of the sermon, but the audience's attachment was by then complete. The purposes of self-esteem and motivation for achievement were well accomplished, if the response of the hearers was any indication at all.

A collateral insight to us writers was, for us, even more significant and memorable.

Behind that "but" was that which canceled out all the rest of his capabilities. But he was a leper . . . We perceive this person to have some difficulty which we scornfully associate with physical appearance, and it negates all else that he or she would be or do. This is Naaman's problem, to be perceived negatively: to have one's contribution in life nullified or negated just because one's understanding of reality is not the same, and because one is perceived as being "less than," and therefore subject to a disregard.

It is important for us to appreciate and understand this, because, you see, another leper did not write this. Had this been written by another leper, "but" would not be there. *"And"* he was a leper would be there. A leper's perspective changes the grammar. If lepers were to write this story, it would sound different. But let those who do not suffer the malady of this condemnation write your story, and you will always be behind the "but." Your definition will always be behind the conjunction of contravention. "But!" It makes no difference, but . . . It's dangerous to let somebody else write your story. It's dangerous to let somebody else define your existence. We've got to write our story ourselves, if it is to be told properly.

I wonder what it would sound like if lepers had written down Naaman's story. I wonder what kind of compassion would have attended this designation, had lepers written it. I wonder what kind of understanding might have seeped into Naaman's condition of existence had somebody else written the story. It doesn't mean that he wouldn't have submitted himself to the healing waters of the river, but it does mean that the perception about him might have been utterly different. There is this understanding that when one is disadvantaged and disregarded, there is need to have one's own story told by those who understand that condition of existence. And not until that is done, and done with faithfulness, can the true cause of the condition be put before persons.*

I found it hard even to imagine a more appropriate way to motivate the work of that body of writers. The group identification had been complete, on the basis of broad parallels of existence. When this thrust was made, we were completely open to it and moved toward our purposes of writing with great joy and celebration.

The next example of group study focuses on the family of Timothy. The portion presented here is not the complete sermon; the balance of the sermon was a set of parallels for motivating underprivileged youth to their highest possible achievement, by celebrating the resources they already have.

STIR UP THE GIFT

> When I call to remembrance the unfeigned faith that is in thee, which dwelt first in thy grandmother Lois, and thy mother Eunice; and I am persuaded that in thee also. Wherefore I put thee in remembrance that thou stir up the gift of God, which is in thee by the putting on of my hands. For God hath not given us the spirit of fear; but of power, and of love, and of a sound mind.
> *(II Tim. 1:5-7)*

In order to get a better grasp of what this text might be saying to us, I invite you to join me in what might be called a case study of the Timothy family. It's like Bible detective work.

Lois and Eunice, Timothy's grandmother and mother, are mentioned in glowing terms as great Christians. Paul calls to remembrance their sincere faith. This is an almost unparalleled compliment. Yet they had not *always* been in the faith. It would appear that as members of the Diaspora, the dispersion of the Jews beyond Palestine after the fall of Jerusalem, Lois and Eunice had gotten somewhat ashamed of their Jewish heritage. Theirs was a minority race, a minority culture, and a minority religion in Lystra, or

---

* Transcribed from the sermon as preached without a manuscript, November 27, 1987.

wherever they actually lived in Asia Minor. So they took names from the prevailing culture, which was Greek. Eunice was a *Greek* name. She also took a Greek husband; no serious *Jew* would do this. There is every reason to believe that she had no desire to be known or identified as a Jew.

They were "passing" for members of the majority, so to speak. This was so much so that they did not bother to circumcise Timothy, as every true son of the law should have been. He had no telltale marks of Jewish heritage like circumcision. We know this because Paul had to have him circumcised before he could expect him to be effective in the work he sent him to do in Corinth.

They also gave Timotheus a Greek name. This not only made him like his folks; it also pointed him in the Greek direction in terms of self-image. People name their children after what they hope they will be, and one of the most telling descriptions of our time is the fact that people no longer give their children Bible names. They go for football stars and movie actors and actresses. I like the Hispanic habit of naming children *Jesus*. They are not ashamed of that name. Timothy's name means one who honors God, but Lois and Eunice were not ready for an Isaiah or a Jacob. Up to the time Tim was born, they were still in this mode of identifying with the Gentile majority, and they wanted him to think of himself as Greek.

All we can say from this point is that something world-shaking must have happened to Lois and Eunice. By the time Timothy was in his late teens or early twenties, they had established themselves as fearless, unashamed Christians. They were willing to suffer not only as Jews, but also as members of the even more persecuted sect of the Jews, namely the Jewish Christians. Thus Timothy had been exposed to the Christian faith throughout his formative years to such an extent that Paul could say of him that he should be an example to *everybody* in the faith, old and young (I Tim. 4:12). Paul felt confident in sending Timothy to the hardest church on his circuit, Corinth, because he had grown up in a family that was Christian "to the bone."

Now his family heritage was not all Timothy had to offer, in the sight of his mentor, Paul. Paul must have been seeing a great advantage in Timothy's competence in Greek language and culture. In addition, he was just naturally gifted; he was smart. Moreover, he had his own deeply rooted personal faith, experienced in the warm manner of his Hebrew roots. Do you realize what he had? He had the best of *two* worlds, two major cultures and world views. Now that's a tremendous combination.

Paul was keenly aware of this because of his own experience. He himself had been subpoenaed by God to do the same kind of witnessing to the Greek-speaking Gentiles. The original apostles were largely unlettered speakers of Aramaic, and the gospel had to be bridged out of their insular limitations. When a hellenistic Jew was considered as a replacement for Judas, they passed over him in favor of another like unto themselves. They blamed the choice on the straws they were drawing, but I have my suspicions. The Christian faith could never be a world-class religion with his parochial bunch.

In effect, God said that since they wouldn't take this Greek-speaking candidate for the board, the best thing to do was arrest one. So one day on the Damascus Road, God stopped the smartest man available, struck him from his mule, shook him up real good, and blinded him for a while. That was how

God acquired the services of the most gifted writer of the New Testament, and Paul knew very well that *some*body would have to carry on when he had gone.

So Paul told Timothy, the gifted, multicultural whiz-kid of the early church, that he had no reason to be afraid. God had given him gifts far beyond those of the folks with only one culture and no family background. He must stir these gifts up, for God had not given him the spirit of fear, but of power, and of love, and of a sound mind.

The final example is taken from a sermon preached many times under the title, "To Teach Them Diligently." It has been directed to parents as a group, facing the ravages of urbanization, secularization, materialism, and affluence among our young. This version of it is a condensation of the theme sermon of a thirteen-week summer series on NBC's "National Radio Pulpit," in 1978.

TO TEACH THEM DILIGENTLY

And these words, which I command thee this day, shall be in thine heart: And thou shalt teach them diligently unto thy children, and shalt talk of them when thou sittest in thine house, and when thou walkest by the way, and when thou liest down, and when thou risest up.

(Deut. 6:6-7)

A popular pastime in America today is the lamentation of lost traditions. None is more lamented than the widespread loss of deep faith, which nourished integrity and gave great strength in life's storms. Now it may be that this tradition never *was* so pervasive as folks say it was, but even if it is only nostalgic exaggeration, we still need desperately what it represented. So I want to share with you Bible affirmations that I have believed all my life, because they still have remarkable power. They got lost because they weren't passed on adequately. Since *every* life is lived by *some* kind of religion, we have in place of the old tradition a "folk" faith dictated by the mass media and oriented to the selling of material things. It's a religion of getting and supposedly enjoying, to the exclusion of almost everything else.

Today we need to get equal time in the hearts and minds of our children. This is no new problem. Moses' priests had it when they recorded our text. Now of course, these priests didn't have to compete with television, but the religion of the wilderness was threatened by the constant exposure of their young to the materially superior culture of the Promised Land. While the Canaanites enjoyed guaranteed sun and water, which enabled them to *predict* successful crops, the Hebrew culture depended on wild game and plants and prayer. The Canaanites were well-nourished, *beautiful* people. The young Israelites were bound to see how much more attractive their neighbors were and to hate Hebrew food rules.

Look again at these nomads, with ragged skins for clothing, while the Canaanites had linen dyed in elegant patterns. But that's not all; they lived in fabulous houses of stone and mortar, with windows to catch the breeze. Who could ever again appreciate *any*thing associated with tents? They even had a more attractive religion, built around agriculture, with lots of wine and dancing and sensuous rites at their feasts. Hebrews might have won control of the land, but they were losing where it counted, in culture and religion.

As the Hebrews settled into the Promised Land and grew more comfortable, however, the big question became how to stay as close to God in this comfort as they had been in the wilderness. The priests advocated a saturation of their comfortable homes with consciousness of God's presence, word, and will. Parents were to talk about God at *every* opportunity, but *naturally*, in the midst of the flow of life, in *pleasant* ways: "When you are out walking or sitting at the table." Parents were urged to express their faith and insights in the very verses of the Bible: "These words which I command thee." In a word, they were to be so happily and casually full of their trust and values, that every single minute they were with their young would be a teaching moment. You see, they realized that the unspoken and subtle things they *did* were teaching what they really believed, even better than what they *said*. And so it is with us today. Parenting hasn't changed much.

The problem is not one of having so much time that we overindoctrinate; it is trying to compete with the time and influence which the prevailing culture already has. If we don't use every second, our children don't have a choice. They can't choose a faith they have never encountered, and this world will do its best to see that they don't. Parents at most can only manage to keep alive the option of serving God in this world's majority of mammon.

Parents may be overwhelmed by so constant a task, but who is more handily positioned to teach our children? And if the words are, like the text says, *in our hearts,* how can we avoid teaching them every minute of our lives? We only have to spend more time with our children and be more intentional.

I have said I was raised in this tradition. I can recall many experiences in which my folks shared their faith in Bible terms. Daddy wasn't terribly pious, but he taught a lot of good religion. He was a humorist to the end, but the faith in his very bones was always leaking out.

One day we were planting our vegetable garden down by the tracks. At some seven years old, I was busy planting corn, one kernel in each hill. Dad insisted that I put in three or four. "Why?" I wanted to know. "It only takes one." His natural and immediate reply was, "They that sow sparingly shall reap sparingly." Not all kernels were alive, and good farmers avoided depending on only one. I left a few the way I had them, and found out he was right. The way he handled it, I had no inclination to resist it as a biblical authoritarian interruption into my life.

Years later I was a Boy Scout, and Dad was the leader on our camping trips. On my very first trip, I conspired with some friends to plant pepper under selected persons' noses in the middle of the night. Dad was among the elect. Their sneezing was oh *so* funny! There was only one trouble. The time came when *I* was selected for a prank. It was so traumatic that I yet can't recall what it was, but I will never forget Dad's response. I ran to him crying, and he had a great laugh. Then he waved his finger and declared, ''Be not deceived; God is not mocked: for whatso*ever* a man soweth, that shall he also reap'' (Gal. 6:7, emphasis added). The twinkle in his eye told me that he knew who had put that pepper under his nose. And the whole experience helped me not only to remember the Word, but also to understand it with uncommon clarity. Lessons with such concrete audiovisual assistance are etched in little boys' souls.

That must be why the priests suggested chatting about our faith in the midst of real life, rather than depending primarily on formal pedagogy: ''Thou shalt talk of them when thou sittest in thine house, and when thou walkest by the way, and when thou liest down, and when thou risest up.''

I can't resist telling one more of these tales. It was the year of the great crash on Wall Street, but we had our own tragedy. Dad was sick for three months. As Christmas approached, we three Mitchell brothers had a summit conference and concluded that Santa Claus did not apply to us. We were steeled to accept whatever came, and tried to be satisfied that we still had our Dad. We went downstairs Christmas morning, jaws tight and determined to be little men. We were completely unprepared for what we saw: a rather large box for each of us. Our aunt and uncle had decided to brighten our Christmas with a pair of skates each. We could hardly contain our joy.

Once again, Dad was busy interpreting what was happening in the words of the Bible, but this time he wasn't laughing. With joy in his heart and a lump in his throat, he declared, ''I have been young, and *now* am old; yet have I not seen the righteous forsaken, nor his seed begging bread'' (Ps. 37:25).* It was a bit heavy for little boys, but we understood. And I've never had to memorize that verse. Who could forget it after such an experience?

Praise God for pleasant parents who use any time and place to teach the Word! Thank God for saints who equip youth to face life with irresistibly memorable verses! Praise God for folks who just naturally speak interesting bible-ese! Those priests were right. ''Talk about it and live it when you are sitting at home, and when you are out walking; when you are getting up in the morning, and when you are going to bed at night.''

Amen.

Across the nation I have seen audiences identify with the beleaguered Hebrew parents and with mine, building to a celebration of group identity and potential seldom equaled in authenticity and intensity.

---

* Note: This will always be one of the most meaningful moments of my life. But I have seen enough starvation among the righteous on other continents and in America to have serious misgivings about taking this verse as a text for a sermon. I *have* seen ''his seed begging bread'' in recent years.

CHAPTER 9

METAPHORS, SIMILES, AND ANALOGS

We come now to another of what we have been calling "*a* genre," but this one consists in a whole assortment of figures of speech. Their function in common is usefulness by parallel, between things easily seen and grasped, and things which can be stated directly only by abstraction. In the Gospels they are called parables, and Matthew says that "without a parable spake he [Jesus] not unto them" (13:34). These figures of speech include similes, extended similes, simple metaphors, single parabolic sayings, narrative parables, analogs, transitional forms, and so on. Actually, the genres already covered may all be said to function similarly, explicating abstract principle by means of a concrete process, action, relation, object, or whatever. The complexities of metaphoric theory confront us in this particular chapter because the very word *metaphor* now demands it. Whatever one calls these uses, parables or something else, all were practiced by Jesus, and in each case, some concrete entity was employed to explicate truth and motivate response.

In his own way Jesus was following the pedagogic tradition of the Hebrew rabbis. He started as they did, with "to what shall I liken this?" But he rose to heights of inspiration and motivation that exceeded the goals of the great rabbinic tradition of taletelling and parables. Rabbis were interested in the way story-symbols facilitated their teaching and debates on the Law. They were realistically aware that images help comprehension and retention far better than abstract statements. Jesus was equally concerned about clarity, but he went beyond this to employ vividness and drama to bring about growth in the hearer. He had a behavioral purpose also. Thus the good Samaritan story not only answered a question concerning the Law; Jesus planned his characterization to expand meanings and motivate compassion.

In recent years the role assignment given metaphors by the rabbis has been supplemented by considerable hermeneutic explorations. Sallie McFague TeSelle starts with the rabbinic assignment of parables as source of theology (*Speaking,* p. 2), but moves on to parables as a *way of knowing* (p. 4), as well as a way of communicating. This is accomplished by the use of the familiar, but more than the familiar is communicated. "The kingdom [the unfamiliar] is a coin which a woman lost and found. . . . *New* meaning is generated by making words mean more than they ordinarily do: this, in fact, is the definition of metaphor" (p. 16). Although one may not deny the rabbis all credit for having fresh insights, it is certain that Jesus was likewise bent on new, radical meanings. And it is certain that those meanings for today are well nigh inexhaustible, as well as relevant to life.

Many other scholars have come forth with ideas similar to McFague's firm contention that "metaphor creates the new, it does not embellish the old, and it accomplishes this through seeing similarity in dissimilars" (p. 49). Paul Ricoeur has explored this extensively, and goes so far as to say that metaphor is a medium of fresh *revelation.* To the role of new meaning he would add the role of *redefining reality (Semeia,* p. 75). All of this occurs as a result of the tension (sometimes referred to as the absurdity or semantic impertinence) between the terms of a metaphorical statement (pp. 77-78). The terms are more than substitutes; more than registering the obvious, they *create* resemblances (p. 79). By moving beyond ordinary meanings, one is freed to form a new world. "A memorable metaphor has the power of cognitively and affectively relating two separate domains by using language appropriate to the one as a lens for seeing the other" (p. 85).

It is at this point that one can begin to see the relationship between these scholars and this work on homiletics. Both affirm the whole of human consciousness, so important in this approach to preaching. The cognitive is not their exclusive goal for hermeneutics. McFague pointedly declares, for instance, that the term *father* in the Parable of the Prodigal Son is emotionally charged and prone to influence *feelings* about God (*Speaking,* p. 44). Ricoeur goes on beyond this sort of impact, but concedes that the traditional rhetorical role of metaphor is as an ornament of discourse with an *emotional* function (*Semeia,* p. 77). And, of course, all rhetoric is for the purpose of persuasion (p. 76).

Ricoeur's insistence on going beyond flat and obvious meanings is an important contribution. His revolutionary hermeneutic savors the outrageousness of the love of the prodigal son's father, or his shocking willingness to disburse his son's portion of the inheritance *before* his own death. Imagine actually honoring that wastrel on his return!

Again, how could any preacher deny that the awesomely radical meanings of the Parable of the Laborers and the Hours (Matt. 20:1-16) must be addressed? They must be made effective in hearers' lives, the more because they are so difficult and world-changing. Indeed, the final, celebrative response due the gospel may well be in proportion to the extent that the *"news"* is just that unexpectedly different from the usual, and just that joyously *"good."*

So hermeneutics and homiletics both affirm all of consciousness and, also, have relatively similar goals of changing lives, individually and corporately. The fresh meanings of the former only add to the challenges to be faced in the latter's agenda of being used of the Holy Spirit to change life. In comparison, it might be said that hermeneutics helps set the goals of homiletics, but homiletics emphasizes the methodology of the preaching event.

In this vein the rest of this chapter seeks to enrich preaching by exemplifying the various metaphors and other figures of speech. We shall not be concerned to designate or distinguish between them. For our purposes, suffice it to say that each of those just mentioned involves some kind of concrete comparison. In each case there is a visible entity which in some sense can be thought of as parallel or analogous to some aspect of the gospel truth and its challenge. For short we shall simply use the word *figure* to refer to the whole phrase, "figures of speech," employed above.

Whatever the technicalities of form and nomenclature, and the differences of opinion on what is and is not a parable, the concrete figure is used to assist hearers both in understanding truth, and in identifying into or being engaged by it. Underlying the effectiveness of the figure is familiarity—the power of personal association, of generating self-recognition. This familiarity makes it safe to open up one's psychic-spiritual depths, and comfortable—even enjoyable—to venture "aboard" the experiential encounter being offered, whether brief or extended.

In all candor, it must be conceded that not all parables will be as loaded with meaning, old and new, as the Parable of the Prodigal Son. But all properly chosen figures can be used by the Holy Spirit, just as they were used by our Lord. These figurative usages will speak beyond the richness of fresh insight to generate holistic, life-changing experiential encounters with the truths of the gospel.

One other factor is deeply significant: Figures affirm the significance and sacredness of common people and things. Jesus' use of a seed or a sheep is so powerful partly because it strengthens the bond between himself and persons associated with seeds and sheep. It suggests that all of these things are important to God, and that there is a kind of sacrament to everyday toils and duties. Jesus' employment of a coin or a vineyard bespeaks his own deep identification with the common people and their possessions and pains. It communicates the perpetual presence of the Holy.

After hearing the parable of the radiator, mentioned in chapter 2, auto mechanics and those who just dabbled in fixing their own cars could engage in their work with a fresh appreciation of themselves and their task. What may have been mere occupations became vocations, and their lives of faith and work became a single, seamless tapestry of meaning, no longer rent into the holy and the unholy, the sacred and the secular.

The first example of a figure presented here is the last third of a sermon by Nathan Dell of Richmond, Virginia. Preached to a chapel full of seminary students, it evoked powerful association, and fresh, healing insights and attitudes concerning, among other things, their work of rigorous study in the seminary. The graduation list was the figure employed, and the genius of the sermon was his vivid recall of a simple and widely shared experience among students nearing the end of their studies and approaching the practice of the ministry.

NEW GROUNDS FOR REJOICING

> The seventy returned again with joy, saying, Lord, even the devils are subject unto us through thy name. Notwithstanding in this rejoice not, that the spirits are subject unto you; but rather rejoice, because your names are written in heaven.
> *(Luke 10:17, 20)*

As we read the Gospels, we find very few disciples who were able to open blind eyes with a touch, very few who commanded death to take leave of someone it had captured, very few who could cool fevers or drive evil spirits from confused minds. There is a James and John here, a Deborah or a Lydia there, but most of us serve the Lord with minimal capabilities, low-to-normal spiritual gifts, and minimal "success." And there are many faithful souls who never ever see any success at all.

The Lord Jesus knows that if achievement or success becomes the main well-spring of our Christian joy, too many Christians will not rejoice at all. So look at what Jesus does. He shows us that the chief ground for rejoicing is a gift within reach of all of us. He makes it possible for *every* believer to have her or his name recorded on heaven's family register. John (1:12) wrote that "as many as received him, to them gave he power to become the sons of God, even to them that believe on his name.'' Not to all who are gifted . . . not to all with large abilities . . . not to all with outstanding achievements . . . not to all with great spiritual endowments, but to as many as received him and believed on his name. If you and I do not have any unusual spiritual or other feats and powers, it's all right. We can still be enrolled in the family of God.

This inspires a rejoicing that goes beyond the satisfactions of impressive gifts and monumental accomplishments. After all, when we have rendered our highest service and attained the greatest superiority in our work, we still find ourselves to be but ''unprofitable servants.'' So what*ever* the success our hands and hearts have known in his name, we shall rejoice. Not chiefly that the very demons were subject to us, but in this that our names are written in heaven. Well did the old hymn raise the penetrating question:

> Is my name written there,
> On the page white and fair.
> In the book of Thy kingdom,
> Is my name written there?
> (Mary A. Kidder)

When I was a student at Savannah State College, near the end of the final semester, the Registrar's office would post, on a bulletin board in the lobby of the administration building, a list of the students who could expect to graduate. You should have seen us crowding around that place, trying to get a glimpse of our names. If your name was not on the board, you would not be allowed to graduate at that June's commencement. If your name was not written there, you could not march with your class.

It was not hard to tell the students who did not see their names. They would walk away, some crying, others silent, sad, eyes straight ahead or glued to the floor . . . too embarrassed to look you in the face.

But then there were those who saw their names on the list. Their gladness would not allow them to keep silence nor remain still. There was a shout on their lips, a leap in their legs, and a light on their faces. Their names were written on the graduation rolls!

They went back to their studies invigorated and renewed. They still had to finish clearing up the bills they owed the college, but that was all right now, because their names were written in the ''book'' of graduation. They still had to attend classes and finish term papers and take final exams. But none of that mattered now; the board in the hallway bore their names.

I wonder if *your* name is written in the registry of the family of heaven? Have you so received the Lord in your life, so trusted and obeyed that your full name is unmistakably inscribed in the Lamb's book of life? Have you so studied and fulfilled your call to preparation that your name is on that list of those both called and obeying? You don't have to receive honors; it's just that if you can say yes, it will make a great difference.

I know it makes a difference with me. Whatever duties remain, I can perform them; my name's written in heaven. Whatever burdens are left, I can carry them with enthusiasm; you see, I have been informed that my name is on the list up there. Whatever difficulties are required yet to be faced, I can deal with them. My surname and given name both are inscribed in that beautiful book. Life's problems may still be complex, but I can handle the situation with God's help.

I can keep the faith now, even if I can't keep the pace, because my final finish is firm. I can finish this course now, even if I'm sick and can't get well. If my tongue never was very powerful and even if I lose my speech, I have an inheritance on the books over on the other side, and I'll hold out until I get there. If I have worked no miracles and moved no mountains, and even if I can't move one side of my own body, it's all right. My rejoicing is undimmed and my happiness in the Lord is complete. As Jesus said, I can indeed rejoice in that my name is written in heaven. Amen. Amen.

The next example of the use of a figure is taken from a sermon series on self-esteem I have done across the country. This particular sermon addresses the ravages of self-hatred born of conditions of origin, such as small towns and poverty. The first part of the sermon, which is all that is presented here, lays the foundation for self-acceptance by use of the manger of Bethlehem as a figure symbolizing beginnings from the socioeconomic bottom.

BETHLEHEM REVISITED
or
ON STARTING FROM THE BOTTOM

And she brought forth her firstborn son, and wrapped him in swaddling clothes, and laid him in a manger; because there was no room for them in the inn.

(Luke 2:7)

I know Christmas is over, and the Babe of Bethlehem is supposed to be seasonal, but come with me again to that little town, will you? This time, let's start from zero, with some new understandings. Let's do away with all sentimentality. In other words, let's not have any more of that "po' little Jesus" stuff this time. And another thing: Let's get off the innkeeper's back. Everybody and their sisters and brothers are in town. With no prior reservation at the "Bethlehem Holiday," you simply don't get a room. This desk clerk or night manager is only doing what he has to do. Mary didn't *get* a room because the desk clerk didn't *have* a room.

Now, of course, I must admit that when I worked in the Deshler-Wallick, fifty years ago, I would hear every now and then of an "important" person who had arrived at the desk with no reservation. When that happened, the alarm would go out, and we would have to *"make"* a room in minutes. But that's a "horse of another color." The people we "built" a room for had money, and they were regular customers. It was the clerk's job to find rooms for people like that. But that clerk in Jesus' day wasn't running an obstetrics ward; the fact that he turned Mary down is not to be construed as meaning that he was a cold-hearted, cruel fellow. We've got to stop this business of giving the innkeeper a bad time.

To tell you the truth, I have no problem with the stable and the manger. A feedbox differs very little from a cradle, except for maybe the rocker. The hay in it is a form of grass, and it's clean and soft and sweet and comfortable. When I was a kid, I *ate* hay and enjoyed it. That is, I walked through fields and pulled up stalks of hay and ate the bottom inch or so. It was sweet *and* very nourishing. Why worry about the hay?

In fact, why worry about the swaddling clothes? Rich or poor, all any baby ever gets is a diaper. There are no high fashion diapers or bandages for babies, so far as I know. Have you ever heard of a Brooks Brothers diaper? If today the only choice is between paper disposables and soft, cotton diapers, I'll take the cotton every time. That's a swaddling cloth. Not only do you not need any more than that; a *baby* couldn't use it if the baby had it.

Jesus is not to be pitied. He has five fingers and five toes, all his faculties, two loving parents, and his good health. The cattle aren't going to bother him, and the wise men and shepherds have no problem finding him. So what is there to pity? Now what I am saying here for tonight is, Let's quit pitying Jesus. He may have *looked* as if he was down, but he had everything he really needed.

Furthermore, I have a strong notion that God even *preferred* it this way. And quiet as it's kept, there are many, many advantages to this manger birth.

The Savior of the *world* had to be accessible to *every*body. There is no problem for a king to come down to visit at the bottom, but there would be great protocol problems if the wretched of the earth sought audience in royal circles in order to pay homage to Jesus. No matter how poor we are, or what class we are supposed to be in, we can get to Jesus, the child in the manger.

I might add that the manger is also a *convenient* place for the visitors to get together. These here shepherds are right out of the field, and they haven't had time to bathe and shave. They are dressed for the field, and they have been sleeping there for days. I know of no other place where these two groups, royalty and rough-hewn shepherds, could find common ground. You see what I mean when I say that the manger has strategic advantages?

Then there is the clarity of perspective that the view from the bottom provides. It's a philosophical advantage; the existentialist philosophers say that if you want to understand a civilization, ask the slave, don't ask the sovereign. There are two reasons for this. One is that the slave is at the bottom, so that he can look in one upward direction and see the whole thing. The other is that he has nothing to lose by telling the truth. If the report comes from half way up, there may be advantages to protect. And it may cost too much to tell the truth if one is at the top. But if the report comes from the bottom, there is nothing to lose. Being accustomed to that rank, the reporter is apt to say, "I've been down so long, down don't bother me. Tell it like it is!" God wanted the savior of the world to be born in this position of superior wisdom and objectivity.

Since everything God allows can eventually be used for some good purpose, I keep looking at this manger, and I see God witnessing. The manger speaks to the issue of God's omnipotence and providence. In the manger, God says that all the power to establish the leadership of the earth is finally God's. God is saying, "If I so desire, I can renew the world's leadership from the most unexpected places. No dynasty or tribe or class of people can have a monopoly on the high places of state." God is reminding the powerful people of the earth that they can't give their gifts and power to their children unless the Giver of every good and perfect gift permits it. And *any* child, no matter how illiterate or debauched his or her parents, just *may* be a strategic contributor to the welfare of mankind.

Manger kids can go all the way to the top. In *Black Preaching* (pp. 131-32), I quote Gardner C. Taylor's recall of an experience of meeting a friend from childhood. The man had come from poor, illiterate, share-cropper parents, and he had many times almost had to leave college and medical school because of a series of financial crises. But he had never given up, and God had given him great gifts, and provided for his needs. When they met this time, he was professor in a medical school. God is giving witness that origins do not determine endings, and the author of all the world's intelligence can raise up whomsoever, from mangers and all sorts of other unlikely places.

The crowning detail in this unlikelihood is to be seen in Jesus' family tree. The manger baby's genealogical chart in the first chapter of Matthew offers some interesting data. The charts of that day did not usually record mothers; only fathers. But there are four women here, and they are an unusual group to say the least. Some scholars say God wanted them listed because they were, all of them, non-Jews, which establishes Jesus' ancestry as multi-ethnic. Jesus has blood ties outside the Hebrew race and in this sense is the more the savior of the world.

But there is something even more unlikely here than non-Hebrew ancestry. Thamar in verse 3 had to resort to strange tactics to guarantee an heir for her late husband. She played the part of a prostitute. Next, in verse 5, comes Rachab (Rahab), the ally of the scouts of Israel and elected to the Hebrews' Hall of Spiritual Fame (ch. 11). She actually *was* a prostitute, yet she is also David's great-great-grandmother. Her daughter-in-law was Ruth, the mother of Obed and grandmother of Jesse. Her way of seeking a husband would raise some eyebrows. Then there is this mention of Solomon's mother, Bathsheba. Whatever scholars may think of this genealogy, it is clear that the evangelist, Matthew, wants it known that the manger baby had what many would consider a less than socially acceptable family tree.

I feel close to Jesus, because his roots are like my roots and the roots of so many I know. And I hear what God is saying to me and the likes of me with this manger: "If the world was saved by a babe born in a manger, you can be proud of your own manger class background. And you can go as high as any man or woman in the kingdom of God."

CHAPTER 10

THE INEVITABLE COMBINATIONS

This final chapter on genres deals with the inevitability of sermons with many genres, all of them fitting definition. Many shorter passages may even qualify for more than one definition, and it may be difficult to say which genre provides the moves for the flow in which the other genres occur. Much has been said already about the fact that few sermons will be found to depend on a single genre for the purpose of generating an experiential encounter with the Word. At the end of chapter 2, we also confronted the reality that some vehicles defy classification. This is to say that many effective vehicles of communication perform the function of several genres as defined. The issue is not to have a specific name for a vehicle, but to use it effectively to help the Word come alive—to be used of God to help it form in the hearers' consciousness. The Bible account itself is constantly flowing from one channel of symbolic meaning to another.

Such a discipline as conscious precision of focus would have been utterly strange to the folk-thinking of Israel. Yet this kind of intentional function for the various literary genres was always there in the culture, practiced intuitively by the best communicators. No Hebrew would have denied that Israel's history was truly a *purposeful* "salvation history," designed to tell about Israel's deliverance and salvation, *and* to teach the insights needed to *keep* the people of God delivered and whole. It matters not what name one might now give the vehicle of vividness, so long as the goal of the scripture is served.

How, then, does this inevitability of the combination of genres bear on the task of sermon preparation? Once one has spent the proper time at exegetical study and can adequately envision the various vehicles already in the Word, then one can move into a folk modality—casually and spontaneously using the genres as they occur in the natural flow of the preacher's consciousness. One does not have to comply with any preestablished formalities. The assignments of specific genres for a particular class session are over. The challenge is to be free to yield to the floating movements of free association and, one dares to say it, the very guidance of the Holy Spirit. It is at just such times and in just such meditation that the best guidance for vivid portrayal is given.

This kind of "flow" is the lifeline or blood supply of good preaching. But it still has to be carefully reviewed and disciplined before the final edition and the actual delivery, whether from verbatim manuscript or from an outline, or even from good memory. Some guidelines for the purposes of review seem therefore to be quite in order.

The first guideline is: Use no more genres or figures than are absolutely necessary. It is far better to exhaust one, and the Word from which it comes, than to skip lightly through a number of different vehicles, or several examples of the same vehicle, failing in each to achieve its full potential for real encounter. The most common example of this is probably the mixing of metaphors. Of course, there may be times when one figure just simply will not symbolize and express all that one feels led to say. However, the switch should never be made before reaching such limits.

In chapter 12, there is an attempt to deal theologically with the problem of probability and authentic spontaneity in audience response to preaching. The figure used in the discussion is that of farming, taken from I Corinthians 3:1-9. However, this figure does not offer all the shades of meaning necessary to the understanding of a statistically improbable single event in a context of larger groupings of occurrences. To put it bluntly, good crops are more predictable than homiletical impact. A better figure is the baseball batting averages I have heard about all my life. So I beg leave to switch figures. Our labors in the study and pulpit, I say, are like the practice and performance of a batter. They are used of God in God's own time, and we are constantly humbled by the fact that on our own we can never predict exactly when we will have a part in a spiritual hit or a home run. Then back to Paul's agricultural figure.

The moves between figures are clearly marked, which exemplifies a second guideline: Be sure to indicate it clearly when you do have to shift figures. People get lost in between if the change is not signaled. Markers should be easy to hear and understand, but not necessarily long. When Jesus was using a series of figures about the old and the new (Matt. 9:16-17), the next figure was signaled with a simple, "*Neither* do men put new wine into old bottles . . ." Thus did he move from the figure of new patches on old clothes. Moves simply must be indicated clearly but subtly. This is true whatever the genre of the move, even in plain prose.

What must be said of figures, however, does not have to be said concerning changes of genre. In fact, genres have a way of overlapping and of being included inside one another. So one does not usually call attention to the genre in use, or to changes of genre, except to say on occasion that one is reminded of a story or a poem, or a person one once knew, and so forth.

In the sermons that follow, there are combinations of several genres. In "The Other Women," the basic continuity is that of a *narrative*. The story means little, however, without the careful portraits of the characters, so far as we know them. So the women are treated with *character sketches*. The story contains more action than is apparent on its surface. Indeed, the most important action is in the minds of the characters, so the thoughts portrayed come forth as a kind of *stream of consciousness*. In addition to all of this, there is a sense in which the treatment of women as a whole is a *group study,* setting forth issues germane to the characters' action and stream of thought.

One need not self-consciously label everything in first draft, but it helps immeasurably to become aware later of the genres (or combinations and mixtures of genres) during review and edit. The idea is to be sure that each vehicle, however it might be labeled, was developed appropriately, and that it was used to the best advantage. One needs also to become aware, on second reading, of possible symbolic signals not consciously intended. It behooves the preacher to try to be sensitive to all possible reactions in the hearers' minds, as triggered by the richness of well-chosen vehicles.

The inevitability of multiple-genre designations is one more reminder that it is God who gives the increase from the channels we are led to use.

THE OTHER WOMEN

It was Mary Magdalene, and Joanna, and Mary the mother of James, and other women that were with them, which told these things unto the apostles.

(Luke 24:10)

(New Testament lesson: Luke 23:55–24:12)

All of Jesus' followers felt an awful desolation there at Calvary. We don't usually associate it that way, but it was like that feeling which overwhelms the people at the prison gate, after they have struggled against an execution and failed. You see, the crucifixion was just that: an execution. Jesus had received his between two thieves. It was a crushing defeat of all that his disciples had hoped for, and they pretty much left the scene to grieve, probably in private. After all, what was there to talk about now?

However, there was a righteous member of the Sanhedrin Council who had dissented from the verdict of death. He even went so far as to risk the censure of his peers by requesting custody of Jesus' remains, in order to follow the Jewish law and bury him before sundown. To do this he had to provide his own new burial place, carved out of stone. That involved what amounted to a large donation—a capital gift. He may only have followed Jesus afar off, if at all, but his gracious treatment of Jesus more than justified Luke's report that he was a good and just man.

Now although the official male disciples had left the cross, there were some women who stuck around. After they saw what was done with the body, they ran home to prepare some spices for the proper embalming of the remains. As soon as it was lawful, early Sunday morning, they came back, not knowing how they would get the stone rolled from in front of the tomb. To their complete amazement, the stone was already rolled away, and when they ran to look in the tomb, Jesus' body was gone. A couple of angels told them that Jesus was risen, just as he had said he would. So these female followers had to run back to town and look up the disciples and tell them that Jesus was risen.

Thus endeth the traditional and beautiful story of the first Easter morn. Now let's look at this apparently "harmless" narrative and identify the dynamite. In the first place, who in the world *are* these women? They must surely belong to *some*body, male that is. And how on earth do they get away with wandering around unprotected, which would mean unguarded? Mark (15:41) agrees with Luke (23:49 and 55) that they are Galilean, women who have apparently been following Jesus for some time, and at some distance from home, since they are all the way down here at Jerusalem.

Now what in heaven's name are they doing together? Common sense would lead me to suspect that they stay together to protect their reputations. But they may have united even more for their protection as the property of their husbands. This sort of a group is *rare,* but they *have* to stick together to follow Jesus at all. Their husbands are not Jesus people, and there is no way the culture will let them join the official band of disciples. Indeed, the women's groups we see today are in existence for pretty much the same kinds of reasons. A lot of husbands still let it be known that they don't want their wives frequenting coed meetings. And it was only a few decades ago that the need for women's national missionary agencies finally ceased. They united with what we call the "parent" body and were given equal status in governance. The struggle is far from over.

Now another question sticks out here. Just what is the difference between the sisters whose names are listed, and the ones referred to as the "other women." Of course, that just means that they are other than the named ones, not what it might mean today. But I am intrigued by the possible reasons for knowing and listing some by name and not others.

The first one named is Mary Magdalene. She has already been mentioned, with Joanna and Mary, in the eighth chapter of Luke's Gospel. He says there that she has had seven demons cast out of her. Now, putting two and two together, I figure that her gratitude knows no bounds, so she gladly travels to Jesus' places of ministry whenever the "girls," as it were, can manage the trip. It also stands to reason that she must have better-than-usual income, and a husband who is likewise glad that she has been healed. Let me state quite clearly that she is *not* the Mary who had been a harlot, but it would have been all right even if she had been the same person.

Then there is Joanna, the wife of Chuza, Herod's steward. If her husband runs the palace, hiring and firing folks, and buying all the provisions, it stands to reason that she is wealthy. She is also quite prominent, and I am inclined to wonder just what Jesus did for her that makes her willing to go to such lengths to follow him. Dr. Luke apparently doesn't know either, or he would tell us. In fact, all that he tells us is about her husband, which is just about par for the course. People still seem to think a woman has to have a husband to have any identity in the world.

Finally, there is Mary, mother of James the younger, and also of Joses or Joseph (according to Mark). Matthew says she is the mother of Zebedee's children, but in any case she shares with the other two named ladies the fact that she has enough means to travel, and the fact that she is defined by the men in her life: her sons.

That brings us to the question of why only these three are named and the others are not. Off the top of my head, I am guessing that they are local folks, but the Gospel writers all agree that the entire group are Galileans. The best evidence available seems to be Luke 24:1, which says that *they* came bringing spices, and the *others* came with them. That suggests that maybe the named three have more money than the others, and can afford the expensive spices to be used for the belated embalming. This figures; even in a male dominated world, women are given *some* recognition if they control some money. True, they must all have been better off than most folks, just to be able to move about, but there are apparent economic distinctions among them.

Would you bear with me for one more question? It has to do with Luke. You see, he is usually much more sensitive to the concerns of women and children than are the other writers. Check it out. But here he groups these women without their names in a way never applied to men. Paul may speak of Jesus being seen of Cephas and five hundred brethren (I Cor. 15:4-6), but Luke *names* men. The only answer would seem to be that even though Dr. Luke is more open to women's rightful interests than most men of his day, he is not perfect by any means. He is, to at least some extent, still a creature of his culture.

Now let's get on once again with the story. These Galilean women are set to go all the way with Jesus. When the others have left the dismal scene of apparent defeat, they stay on and keep watch over the remains of their Lord. It seems the least that they can do. They watch and perhaps help Joseph of Aramathea, as he takes the body down, wraps it in linen, and carries it to his new tomb.

But wait! These are *respectable* women, and the touching of the dead is supposed to *defile* you. High priests are completely forbidden to touch the corpses of even their own daddies! It takes seven whole days to get cleansed after you have touched a dead body. *Ladies* ought not to defile themselves.

But they don't hear a word of it. This is their *Lord,* and they couldn't care less about the ritual rules of defilement. This may be even more risky than staying away from home, but so what? They will stick as close as they can, as long as they can. The only reason they don't embalm him this same Friday evening is that darkness is overtaking them, and it is Sabbath. And they haven't even had time to go to the market.

The very first opportunity after that is sun-up on the first day of the week, and they are right there at the crack of dawn. They have bought and brought their spices, and they are fully prepared to go to work, to see to it that the indignity of a criminal's death is not matched by a denial of the amenities of a dignified burial. Watch them as they make their way, pushing the rule a bit and hiking in the near darkness. Jesus is officially dead, but they can't wait to offer whatever amenities they may be able to offer.

All the while they are wondering how they will roll the stone away, but lookie here! The stone is already moved, and the tomb is wide open. They rush in, and, *wow,* no body! They are about to tear their hair with grief and perplexity, when two men in shining garments appear, and remind them that the Lord had said it would be like this before they left Galilee. They are quite stunned at first, but suddenly they realize the glory of it all, and they rush back to town to tell the disciples. Their joy borders on the unbearable. "He is risen, even as he said!" There has never been nor will there ever be any greater joy than this. With or without names in the record, this has to be the most exciting moment and the most important news ever!

As I look back, I have to marvel at the very existence of this group. They are not self-conscious nonconformists, or feminist radicals aforetime. They are just women whom Jesus has healed and liberated, and on whom he has bestowed respect. Here is this woman whom Jesus has delivered of seven demons now serving as the obvious *leader.* Luke (8:2) says that *all* of them have been cured of *some*thing. Who knows? One may have had an issue of blood (8:43ff.) and another may have been bent over for eighteen years (13:11ff.). Neither can forget that he touched her, and broke all the rules in order to heal and free her and give her hope. They were there because they loved the Lord, and they were quite literally united in Christ.

Their gratitude and human sensitivity would not let them leave the job until it was properly and compassionately completed. There were no "minutes" of the women's society, no budget, no officers, no struggles for power or the prominence of office. Only the love of Christ sprang irrepressibly in their breasts at this point. Yes, the work was supposedly dirty and demeaning in the eyes of their community, but it had to be done. It was disgraceful not to be "properly" buried, so it probably didn't occur to them to worry about uncleanness. The Kingdom's business requires attitudes like this sometimes.

If we, male or female, shy away from unpleasant, dirty tasks, we can't look for a promotion from our God, who requires us to be "faithful in *little* things." If God sends us to "unclean" addicts and AIDS patients, that's where the action in God's name begins today. Jesus washed feet and touched lepers and used a substance we call spit.

I am reminded that my own mother had some tales like this to tell. She was church missionary–social worker during World War I. She worked among the people brought to town in cattle cars, to work in the armaments factories. They lived as they came, for there were no houses for them. So she walked the alleys late at night and changed diapers in converted garages and barns. She did laundry and cooked on makeshift stoves. It was risky for a young woman, but she didn't seem to know that at the time. The war ended, and in later years I never heard my home church say a word about what Mama did.

This morning I can't promise you any more headlines than Mama got for her labors. She was one of those "other women" like the ones you find in the Bible. And you, like millions of others, may be one of those other women too. Pastors, deacons, trustees, and others may have to stand trial for the way they have exploited and ignored women in some churches, but faithful work cannot be obliterated. Matthew, Mark, Luke, *and* John had to say *some*thing about such. You may never get a gavel or a plaque, or even a bouquet of flowers or your name in the bulletin, but God knows, and the best records of our time will have to do likewise unto you. What you do for Jesus will in some way "leak out." You see, God exercises the right to squeeze a blessing out of even the worst of injustices, after we have done all we can to remove them. You'll never ever regret the work you did, or miss too much the recognition. Just watch!

I think it is inspired imagination that makes me hear the mind of God, as it were, pondering: What shall I do for these anonymous benefactors of my only begotten Son? How may I go about saying just a little of how I am pleased by their quiet, loyal ministrations? What kind of spiritual gift would be truly appropriate to persons of such great sensitivity?

Fortunately, all four Gospels have unanimously answered the question. They say that God must have decided on this wise: Let them have the quiet honor and glorious joy of being first to tell the news that Christ is risen. Let them be the first to announce the Resurrection. They may not let them preach again for centuries, but they'll surely preach the first sermon of the new dispensation. Ladies, the credit is yours, with My blessing!

I don't know what God will do in Cleveland or Philadelphia or anywhere else, but God is still just, and God still works in mysterious ways. Incidentally, you may be interested to know what God did with Mom. Nobody that I can recall extolled her heroic work in my home town, but I love to go to the church in Berkeley, California, where she spent her last years. Bulletins report the meeting dates of the "Bertha Mitchell Women's Missionary Circle." I just love to hear one member casually state, "That old lady taught us all we know about missions, and it's only right that we should name the circle after her." She's dead right! Let us all pray that we will never ever fail to recognize and encourage the quiet ministries we see from time to time.

It was Mary Magdalene, and Joanna, and Mary the mother of James, and all those other women who were with them that told the news to the apostles. And we are compassed about with a host of still other women without name—mothers and grandmothers and wives and sisters and daughters who *still* tell the news and live it out, to the glory of God and the help of us all. Thank God for every last one of them! Praise God for that nameless host and for their valiant ministries! Amen! Amen!

The celebration here is only one of many ways to "be glad about" the work of these unnamed women. Just as whole sermons may have many genres, so may the celebration be approached with great variety. In my culture, the celebration for "The Other Women" would be greatly elaborated; in other cultures it may be appropriate to be a bit less expressive. Suffice it to say that the lasting influence of any sermon will be largely according to the authenticity of the celebration, which means that great care must be given to developing it to the maximum in a given culture.

In the following sermon, the celebration appears equally low key in print, but there is a great deal of flexibility possible. Some of it could be in repetitions for emphasis, as in the preceding sermon, and much depends on the style of the delivery. In the case of this sermon, "A Man After God's Own Heart," there is a highly celebrative phrase in the 15th verse of the Fifty-first psalm: "O Lord, open thou my lips; and my mouth shall shew forth thy praise." Although it was not used as transcribed here, it offers great celebrative possibilities, possibly moved to the end.

The overall structure of the sermon is that of an imaginary *dialogue*. The material involves the serious exegetical research of a *character sketch*. The psalm toward which the whole presentation moves is *stream of consciousness*, and the explanations David gives could easily be labeled brief *narratives*. It is obvious, once again, that it is not essential that something which flows well be forced into the format of one particular genre. The purpose of such classification is simply to shed light on the function of the various approaches in the generating of an encounter of the whole person, leading up to celebrative response and reinforcing growth.

A MAN AFTER GOD'S OWN HEART

Old Testament Readings: I Samuel 16:1-13 and (inside the sermon) Psalm 51
New Testament Reading: Acts 13:14-22

Call this a dream—a vision. You name it. It's something that was given to me.

I was hanging around the halls of heaven and strolling down the streets of gold. As I wandered around one day I saw this handsome, distinguished man. His face seemed so familiar that I got up my nerve and asked, "Sir, somehow I feel I know you. Oh yes, aren't you his royal highness, King David?"

He stopped and smiled almost mischievously, as he said, "I certainly am, and who might you be?"

I was suddenly flustered, but I managed to say, "I'm Henry Mitchell, from Richmond, Virginia."

D Oh, I see, and what did you do there?

H I taught preachers. In fact, I hope to break all the rules and go back and teach some more.

D Pleased to meet you, indeed.

H But I'm *really* pleased to meet *you,* your royal highness.

D Wait, just call me David. Around here we don't use titles. Everybody's the same before the Father. No highnesses, doctors, professors, or other titles—just people. So if you don't mind, I'll also just call you Henry.

H That's great with me; I've always wished it were that way in our churches. Now, uh, David, that makes it easier for me to ask a question that has been haunting me for years. Do you mind me digging into your personal business?

D No, not at all, any more. Just help yourself.

H O.K., David. How's come you were rated as a man after God's own heart, when by law you were a principal accomplice in a cold-blooded murder? And besides, you had a few other pretty heavy offenses, if you don't mind my saying so.

D That's perfectly all right. Help yourself. To tell the truth, I'm still a bit surprised myself at that rating Paul gave me at Antioch. To try to explain it would take quite a while, but if you have the time . . .

H That's about all I *have* got. Please go on.

D Well, to start with, I had no idea that God ever paid me any attention at all until that day they sent for me to come in from the pasture. Then there stood Samuel—that awesome presence! I'll *never* forget *that* day! I was actually filled with the Spirit of God, and I haven't ever been the same since. From then on I knew I was somebody special, with something very important to do in my life. All this even though I was young, and I had never been anywhere, or gone to any school, or even *seen* a king's court. I *still* look back and wonder about how that anointing affected me.

H Is that what gave you the nerve to take on Goliath, when nobody else would?

D Exactly. I wouldn't have dreamed of such a thing, but the Spirit told me that God had to have *some*body, and God refused to be mocked. So I just went on out there. And I told them that was why I was there—in the name of the Lord. But even with all that speech, I was really shocked when he fell so fast. Imagine! That great big man! Dead already!

H Oh you were innocent then, and God could use you any way he wanted to. In fact, I've always admired the high character you showed in the early years. Even when Saul was doing his best to have you killed, you spared his life. You *had* to be after God's own heart when you seemingly weren't even *tempted* to kill Saul, and you had him right there in your hand! You downright refused to get even. You followed that business Jesus talked about later when he told us to love our enemies. You were *so* clean-cut and upright when you were younger! But *some*where along the way you changed.

D   Please! Don't say it with such finality. I did do some terrible things later on, but I never *ever* changed over completely; I just got weak. Now I'm not making excuses, but once I got to be king, it was a lot more complicated than most of you Bible students have any idea of.

H   I'm sure that's true, but Uriah was *killed!* That must have been an awful lot of complication. (Uh, I feel funny calling you David and talking like this.)

D   Go right on. In fact, if you manage to go back to earth, it'll be good that you dug into this and I leveled with you. You're not the only one wondering about that business of my being a man after God's own heart.

H   Thanks! You always were a big-hearted sort of person. But now tell me about those complications.

D   Well, to start with, you have to face the fact that it took *two* of us to get into that mess. Yes, Bathsheba was very beautiful, but she was also very ambitious. Do you remember how anxious she was for *her* son Solomon to succeed me? Well, she didn't just get that way when he was older. She was that way from the start, and she was probably encouraged by her folks. Now, mind you, I didn't fight the feeling, and of *course* I wasn't blind to the political advantages of an alliance with her clan. So that doesn't get me off the hook, but she was *not* taken by violence. . . . Do you understand?

H   I'm afraid I don't. Do you mean she was willing?

D   Not only willing, eager. That whole affair worked out just as that very beautiful lady had in mind.

H   What?

D   Yes. It was no accident that she bathed in clear sight of the place where I walked at night. And she knew just how hard it would be for me to resist the temptation she put out there. Can you imagine yourself a king, able to have whatever, and nobody to challenge you? No police, no news reporters, no supreme court. You *are* the court. . . . One of the closest things in *your* experience would be slave masters. I can *look* at you and tell that *some* master just couldn't resist violating your great-grand-mother. And you understand, he didn't *have* to resist! He was *master!* There was nobody, not even his wife, with power to stop him. It's a lot harder to be pure when you're a king or a master. *Most* people never have to face such powerful enticements.

H   Wow! I begin to get the drift. That's heavy.

D   And let me share with you another small complication. The only reason I sent Uriah to death myself was that he wouldn't take a hint and be weak enough to stay a night with his wife. If he had, he would have been sentenced to death by a *military* court, and I wouldn't have had to touch it. As it was, I *had* to have him die for his country; for if he had lived and this business had spread around, not only I as king but also the country itself would have been destroyed. Nobody else had ever brought Israel and Judah together, and nobody else ever got them back together once they divided after Solomon. He *did* in fact have to die for his country.

H   But wait! Back up, please! You mean Bathsheba was aware that Uriah had to be sacrificed somehow?

D   That's *just* what I mean. How could her father have a grandson who was a king if she were married to dear old Uriah? But don't get me wrong. This does not get me off the hook. As I said, it's just a complication that may help you understand that this whole affair wasn't so strange after all. *Any*body could get started in such a chain of events and wind up a murderer just like me.

H   You know, David, I kinda hate to admit it, but I guess you're right. Now let's get back to the man after God's own heart. You may not be the cold-blooded murderer I wondered about, but that still doesn't put you as high as after God's own heart.

D   You won't get any argument out of me there, Henry, but God used Paul to write more books of the Bible than any other single writer, and he was a chief accomplice in a murder just like me. God works with people as they are. And, too, maybe you should look for a moment at a few of the things I did *right,* besides just refusing to kill God's anointed, old King Saul.

H   Well, everybody knows you were a strong supporter of the Temple and the priesthood. Solomon may have *built* the Temple, but *you* did all the real preparation. Nobody can take that from you.

D   And I seriously tried to do God's will *most* of the time. It may not have seemed so to the man on the street, but I constantly sought the guidance of God in making decisions. I didn't just write it in songs. When I sang phrases like "lead me in the way everlasting" or "lamp unto my feet and light unto my pathway," I *meant* it. I would *never* have been able to govern that huge kingdom without God's guidance. Me a shepherd boy with nothing like formal education! *God* showed me where to look for good ideas.

H   I can see that, but I must admit, I had never thought of it before. The Bible stories make you look like some sort of superman. Most of us Bible students don't associate the spiritually minded author and singer of the psalms with the war hero, rolling them into one human being.

D   I guess that's typical. But let me go on to the bottom line of this "man after God's own heart." I know now that the most important thing I ever did was the way I responded to the pointed finger of the prophet Nathan. All else would have been lost if I had tried to stonewall that one. When he said, "Thou art the man," I nearly died. I had *never* felt that bad in all my life. I fell prostrate before the Lord and fasted and cried. Oh, it was an *awful* feeling. And then when the child died, I hardly knew if I wanted to keep living myself. That's when I got the inspiration for that prayer-hymn, or psalm, as you might call it.

H   You mean the Fifty-first psalm?

D   Yes, I believe that *is* what you folks call it.

H   I sure would love to hear you sing your own song. My, my, my! That would be a *real* blessing!

D   Well, no, not quite. You see, the original music was for a different language, and the music itself was quite different from anything you could relate to. The best way for you to hear it is from your *own* lips and your *own* heart, praying for your *own* forgiveness.

H   I can see now why God loved you so, and you *were* a "man after God's own heart." I can't help feeling very close to you myself—close enough to do just what you said, and pray *your* prayer and mean every word of it. Mind if I get on my knees like I do when I pray for real?

> Have mercy on *me*, O God, according to thy lovingkindness;
> According to the multitude of thy tender mercies
> Blot out *my* transgressions.
> Wash *me* thoroughly from *mine* iniquity,
> And cleanse me from my sin.
> For I acknowledge my transgressions:
> And my sin is ever before me . . .
> Purge me with hyssop, and I shall be clean;
> Wash me, and I shall be cleaner than snow . . .
> Create in me a clean heart, O God,
> And renew a right spirit within me.
> Cast me not away from thy presence;
> And take not thy holy spirit from me.
> Restore unto me the joy of thy salvation;
> And uphold me with thy free spirit.
> Then will I teach transgressors thy ways;
> And sinners shall be converted unto thee . . .
> O Lord, open thou my lips;
> And my mouth shall shew forth thy praise.
> For thou desirest not sacrifice; else would I give it:
> Thou delightest not in burnt offering.
> The sacrifices of God are a broken spirit:
> A broken and a contrite heart,
> O God, thou wilt not despise.

Oh thank you, Lord, thank you! Amen! Amen!

PART III

SOME CONCLUSIONS

CHAPTER 11

THE TRAUMA AND CHALLENGE OF IMPLEMENTATION

This excursion through what, for many, may be an entirely new approach to preaching, has been all too brief. It will need to be fleshed out with many more books and, even more important, years of experience writing sermons designed to generate experiential encounter with and celebration of the Word. This chapter is offered as a summary to clarify the issues and to provide insights to how one proceeds from here, to implement the needed changes.

Many deeply ingrained habits of preparation and patterns of expression will need to be changed. It will not be easy to begin to design vicarious *experiences* and *celebrations of the Word* (highly coherent, of course), when the old habit has always been one of just thinking the points out, period. It is often rather discouraging to face the fact that a coherent outline is only the easiest part; we are just getting started on the sermon at this stage. The real challenge is that of making the ''point'' into a move which helps to form the message in the hearer's consciousness, and which in a natural, easy flow builds to joyous praise. One may feel as though one is starting all over at a late age, and the hard-won habits from previous training may seem much too difficult to break now.

But not to worry; be happy! This could be the means of a resurrection of pulpit and church. And it can happen sooner than one expects, given a clearer understanding, coupled with a prayerful dissolution of a mental block. Underneath that block against a largely new approach is an unconscious resistance to admitting that one has been so far from this mark all these years. The pain diminishes when we face the fact that none of us has a monopoly on this captivity within our culture. Our whole culture has been moving in the same overly cognitive mode. It is also true that there is much of that culture which must be kept and used, so shedding the rest can be easy.

There is actually no pulpit elite in any culture whose excellence is such that we should feel embarrassed. Very often when I look at one of my own sermons from more than two years back, I wonder at how I missed these criteria myself, and I have been teaching preaching for twenty years. There is nothing to do but forget the less effective systems and less carefully formed moves, and press for the mark. We'll all get there sooner than we think. (And let's not call our earlier preaching patterns "errors," for too many folk were blessed in spite of us.) The heights to which we will rise will owe much to many traditions and certainly reflect insights that have come to all of us only recently.

So where does one start on the path to a dynamic, celebrative synthesis of all God has given us collectively, both in the past and in recent years? A first principle might be called *saturation*. Rather than escape the trauma of confronting new systems, move *toward* them and immerse the mind and spirit in them. Read the theories over and over. Then read the applications of the theories as they are found in the sermons provided. *Hear* the sermons as you read, and enter into the vicarious experiences provided. Finally, correlate the moves and other features of the sermon with the theories and principles exemplified.

A second principle involves *disciplined listening* to actual performances of preachers whose theories relate to this experiential-encounter approach. Make it a point to attend services or collect tapes of good examples of the preaching event. Listen to them just for the enjoyment of it part of the time, and then listen analytically, with pen and paper in hand. Without seeking to imitate specific preachers, allow the nuances of formation and flow in consciousness to engulf you as you listen. It will be much easier to write a sermon in this mode, when you have experienced it and allowed it to register in your own depths.

You are then ready to engage in *practice* runs, with or without audiences. The art of preaching is no different from any other art: It requires practice. We do not refrain from preaching in this mode because the first sermon will not be perfect, or live up to expectations. Singers sing to get better. Actors act to improve their performances. And preachers preach in hopes of improvement. I have a habit of telling my classes, called workshops, that I never succeeded in teaching a pupil how to swim without his or her getting in the water. We have to "jump in" to acquire a new preaching pattern.

Once the effort is made, whether before an audience or just before a cassette player, the next move is *self-critique*. The worksheet at the end of chapter 4 is also a checklist for self-evaluation. The discipline of practicing self-criticism can be very productive; the only direction is up, after you make it a lifelong habit. The checklist, however, should be used during preparation, *before* the sermon is delivered, as well as after.

A final word of advice has to do with participation in continuing education *workshops* on the subject. Sharing with others on the same sometimes painful pilgrimage can be very reassuring and encouraging. Not unlike that of groups such as Weight Watchers and Alcoholics Anonymous, there is a camaraderie among those on the quest which provides not only fresh insight but also crucial emotional reinforcement. And remember how many years were required to get the habits which now need reshaping, so as not to demand self-change too rapidly.

It would not surprise me to find that many readers will have at least one other fear to overcome. What on earth is to be done with the congregation during the transition? How does one smooth over the shift from sharp, stimulating essays to these vicarious experiences of the very Word of God? It is generally assumed that the Church of the Living Lord, who changes not, is or ought to be a haven of stability. How much risk is there that one may lose the audience, and even one's position, while dabbling in this new and countercultural communication style?

The first fear of the laity might be that this will reduce creativity and intellectual integrity. But this is far from the actual result, which is to make the insights more relevant. In addition, the new process should increase involvement of the hearer and thus add considerably to interest. Never should one fear that the experiential approach will permit laziness just because the emotions are involved. Quite to the contrary, the emotive factor adds motivation to personal and social change. The challenge is to keep the old amount of content and make it more engaging and life-changing.

Except, perhaps, for such doctrinaire intellectuals as are rarely found in a church, holistic engagement will not be an issue. Unless sermons play on lesser emotions and use them for unworthy goals, most people will welcome the involvement of their whole selves. When this is *not* true, they will complain about the sermon being dry.

Again, warmth and freedom of expression have too often been associated with fuzzy thinking and failure to focus. When animated presentation is both soundly biblical and coherent on the one hand, and clearly directed to some form of growth and development on the other, there can only be gratitude. It is high time the stereotype of a polarity between warmth and truth was over-recorded and outgrown. Truth without holistic involvement, spiritual growth, and serious ethical application is elitist irrelevance, no matter how sound. Holistic involvement without substantive insight is "sound and fury, signifying nothing." The real challenge is not to have either to triumph over the other, but to bring about a powerful, living synthesis of the two. Congregations hunger for such, and few there be who would not praise God for a preacher who could finally bring off the combination.

This whole approach to preaching and worship will still arouse problems of appropriateness in dedicated and sincerely serious minds. In the following chapter, an answer is proposed to the problem of possible manipulativeness inherent in the suggested methods of timed impact. In the area of implementation, there is another possible sincere challenge related to the potential of "charismatic" worship for generating confusion. It cannot be denied that warmly expressive worship draws less reflective minds quite easily. One of the ways we have maintained the "intellectual integrity" of many churches has been to keep worship out of the reach of "crackpots" and excessive enthusiasts by keeping it cold. How does one deal with an invasion of dissimilar congregants, many quite sound and sane, and others maybe borderline, all of them drawn by a more moving and universally attractive gospel?

It should be clear that this is a problem devoutly to be sought, and that there can be solid safeguards against dilution of the sanity of the saints. What we have proposed here was never ever to be construed as free of rigorous and penetrating review processes. Dynamite has to be handled carefully and applied to tasks stringently selected. If God is to bless a less inhibited communication of the gospel, the preacher must be especially careful not to succumb to the temptation to let emotional momentum carry her or him beyond that which is mandated by the Holy Spirit. All too often do pastors and performers in the religious media not only press beyond rightful restraints; they also blame it on the Holy Spirit. It was such a temptation that forced the governing body of America's largest Pentecostal denomination to issue strict warnings and make stern judgments to avoid the appearance of evil in this matter of divine guidance. Their unflinching firmness as responsible charismatics, maintained in the blazing light of the mass media, is a model of the kind of rigorous checks that must accompany all increases in freedom, that it be not the occasion of license.

Among denominational groupings where the decibel output is habitually higher, it must be constantly remembered that sound is not synonymous with soundness. After the spectacles of wind and earthquake and fire, the Lord spake in a still small voice (I Kings 19:12). It may seem contradictory to be so analytical about something so subjective as life in the Holy Spirit, but it is possible and necessary. I John 4:1 states it especially well:

> Beloved, believe not every spirit, but try the spirits whether they are of God: because many false prophets are gone out into the world.

With greater freedom of expression and fuller participation of the person in the experience of the Word, and with stringent care that our new momentum be employed always in the very center of the will of God, the ravages of rampant secularism and materialistic obsession may yet be reversed, and the Kingdom somehow advanced on this planet. It will not be easy for us preachers to make the change to preaching that includes experiential encounter, but it can be done, and it will be worth every bit of the effort required.

CHAPTER 12

THE HOLY SPIRIT AND HOLISTIC PREACHING

A recurrent student concern in my classes through the years has been the need to place this detailed homiletic approach to spiritual depths in theological perspective. Many have believed that it is not the prerogative of the preacher to have anything to do with how the Holy Spirit might reach the heart of the hearer. That hasn't kept them from trying their very best on their own to see that it happened. They simply wanted to be able to say that the Spirit had led them individually. They seemed sincerely to feel, at times, that learning it in a class destroyed the mystery and put the teacher or the book in the holy place where only the Spirit belonged. Many wanted all the help they could get, but they needed a way to fit it into their developing personal doctrines of how God guides the preaching event.

These students' need is not unique; no servant of God, in the pulpit or out, dares ignore the inevitable assumptions on which a whole life's vocation is based. It is all the more important when the spiritual welfare of others may hang on those assumptions. In this book, there are not only theological assumptions but also several psychological assumptions which are very important to this approach to the communication and adequate hearing of the Word. If, as Paul suggests (Rom. 10:14), hearing is crucial to saving faith, considerable theological reflection is needed to clarify the role of the human preacher's efforts and technical-artistic insight in so awesomely important an exercise.

The preacher's task is to provide a *total experience* of the gospel. This is set over against an exclusively cognitive or intellectual grasp of divine truth. The experience-centered gospel is to stimulate the growth of gut-level trust in God by providing vicarious involvements in the *encounters* where faith had and has been caught and taught. In transactional terms, it means being used of God to stimulate the "recording-over" of the intuitive "tapes" of unbelief with new "recordings" of profound trust in God. This message to the intuitive consciousness should be followed by the emotive *celebration* of the gospel truth. This gives ecstatic reinforcement to the comprehension of and dependence on the Word of God. Scholarly support for this approach is growing rapidly. Recent psychological understandings and artistic techniques need to be discerned in proper relationship to the work of the Holy Spirit. At best, the preacher is only an instrument in the hands of God, who saves all the souls that are saved, and who stimulates living faith using catalysts called preachers, who are guided by the Holy Spirit.

Notwithstanding, many a student has risen to ask if this recording-over is a new kind of determinism or divine predestination, with election based on the preacher's skills. They have suspected a kind of behaviorism, void of human will. "So what place does the choice and initiative of the hearer have in this whole process?" Still others have asked for the relationship between salvation and healing, and the place, if any, of sin. If, then, some readers are to give wholehearted attention to the mechanics and technique addressed here, some of these honest questions will have to be examined.

The first clarification of relationship best deals perhaps with salvation. This is often thought of as first in the goals for the preaching of the gospel, followed by healing, growth, and empowerment. Salvation is all the more demanding of attention because, unlike the other three, it is so much less amenable to any sort of verification, or to the tracing of influences on behavior. The purveyors of pat plans of salvation go entirely too far when they purport to speak for God about who is or is not saved, and exactly how or by what spoken formula. Although the "Assurance of Pardon" is an orthodox and patently valid element of traditional liturgy, it is not to be confused with an individual assurance of salvation, based on a glib repetition of a man-made prayer or confession. Equally repugnant would be any remote suggestion that there is a cause-and-effect relationship between the efforts of the preacher, as a learned and compassionate healer, and the salvation of the hearer. Whatever the sensitivity and psychological expertise of the preacher, we are all saved by *grace* through faith (Eph. 2:8), and *no* person will know exactly who else is in that number until the final arrival on the "other side." There will, of course, be those whose gracious manner and glowing spirit will mark them as prime suspects for salvation. They may even have been greatly influenced by some practitioner of preaching who follows the rules suggested here. But there will always be enough folks who appear saved without such ministries, and enough who have heard such to no effect, to keep the greatest artists and healers in the pulpit humble. It will always be God who saves and to whom the glory will be due.

Therefore, we human beings must pray, prepare, and preach *as if* the whole responsibility were on the preacher, but trust, knowing that ultimately the responsibility is God's, no matter how useful or useless our best efforts may appear. As Paul put it, we must plant and water, but God is the one who gives the increase (I Cor. 3:6-8). Some years' crops are bounteous; some are not. And the chief atmospheric causes are in the hands of God.

This figure, however, opens up windows of practical insight. Salvation and the visible *fruits* of wholeness are closely associated. Jesus talked as if the saved "tree" should show forth spiritual health and growth, together with fruitful empowerment for work and witness (Matt. 7:16, 20). Although, in the last analysis, this too is in the hands of God the Holy Spirit, there is a sense in which the effectiveness of the homiletical "cultivation" of the trees is subject to some dependable mode of judgment. One does not have to take part in the American preoccupation with numbers and supposed success to be sensitive to the growing presence or absence of the fruits of the Spirit among one's hearers (Gal. 5:22-23). The use of a dedicated mind and the openness of a spirit to *the* Spirit can, thus, be expected to yield conditions which appear best to be used of God toward the wholeness and growth of persons. One can accumulate awareness of climates in which the Holy Spirit works best and blesses most. Souls and psyches are hard to separate, and the knowledge of the latter may at times be used by the Holy Spirit to gain access to the former.

However, like all figures, that of the fruit tree breaks down, if pushed too far. The best weather for crops can be so carefully calculated that the vintners in California's San Joaquin Valley can know exactly how many very hot nights in a summer are necessary to the proper sugar content in the raisins. It is not thus with the harvest of souls. Even given a certain atmospheric condition, the yield itself is still in the hands of God. If one were to change the figure to a more crude parallel in baseball, this truth would be lifted up more accurately. Although players practice hitting for hours, and although the managers know well that a .350-average hitter is always a better basis for hope of a score, no given hitter can be *sure* of hitting at any given turn at bat. Whether or not there will be a hit, and for how many bases is never within the power of human beings accurately to predict.

There is no exact cause-and-effect relation between the hitter's effort and the result of any given stand at the plate. Success follows a plan beyond any human's precise wisdom.

Nevertheless, every batting coach knows that for certain hitters, certain stances, grips, and swings are more productive than others. The percentages over time reflect the value of good coaching, as well as the genius of the hitter. So it is with the preacher who has followed or will follow the kinds of insight offered here. The glory for the saving and healing and help of the hearers goes to God, but God, by the Holy Spirit, uses the truths of many academic and theological disciplines to fulfill the divine purpose. Indeed, the God of all truth is the author and revealer of all these professional means of reaching and serving human need.

This could raise another challenge emanating from a fractious student or two every decade or so: How dare a professor assume that there is such a discipline as homiletics, and that any mere human can teach another to preach? They commonly assume that what they preach is by the Holy Spirit and between them and God alone. It is outright effrontery to God for a professor to insist on involving a class in the preparation of students' actual sermons to be preached in their pulpits. And this in a required course yet!

In the sense that salvation is of God, they are right, since one does not instruct the Holy Spirit how to act in either hearer or student preacher. Teachers and classes, however, *can* offer suggestions where clearly needed, with the understanding that the Holy Spirit must validate those suggestions if they are to be used in the actual delivery of the sermon. To move the figure back to farming, even though Paul fully recognized that it was God alone who gave the increase, or the harvest of saved souls (I Cor. 3:6), there had to be some planting and watering. It takes training to be a good farmer, even to plant and water. These skills are teachable to open minds. The indispensable value of teaching efforts and of books like this one is that of making better nourishers of the saving and growth of the human spirit. While it is all too obvious that books can go only so far, it is also essential that preachers be sure to go that far—to ask God to intervene only after they have done all they can do. God *expects* the farmhands of the Spirit to exhaust their human resources, at their proper distance from the planted seed, before they look to God to cause that seed to move from death to life.

Once again, however, the figure can be pushed too far. Students have just cause to raise the issue of the place of human will or volition;

seeds have no conscious will. However one resolves the issue of the roles of Holy Spirit and preacher, there is yet the role of the hearer to be considered. Is there not a danger that this idea of over-recording the hearer's intuitive tapes will be seen as a passive and even involuntary experience for the hearer? The answers come from both Scripture and clinic. Jesus required ''clients'' to take some part in the healing. One had to go get his own mud and another had to pick up his bed and walk. No healing at the clinic or the church can take place without the cooperation of the person in need. He or she must come to the clinic in the first place. It is necessary then for the hearer to cooperate in the whole process, and to have openness to and confidence in the healer. So seeds come to life, so to speak, but souls always keep at least a tiny spark of the image of God in which they were made. That irremovable residue, no matter how small, must be mobilized in the saving and healing process. To believe otherwise is to paralyze both pastor and parishioner, since pastors do not normally share the Holy Spirit's power to resurrect the dead.

What has been said in the clinical setting must also be said of the event called preaching: No soul is saved or blessed when not in fact seeking or at least willing somehow to receive the blessing. Even Paul on the Damascus Road was trying to please God, albeit in gross error. People simply cannot be mesmerized into wholeness and a holy life which they refuse to accept. Whether in Alcoholics Anonymous or elsewhere, one has somehow to acknowledge need and express desire. The sermon-generated experience of a gospel truth in some depth has to be *accepted* by the hearer for recording on her or his own intuitive tapes. One has the option to reject. Although, of course, it is true that one preacher may make acceptance far more attractive than another can, no preacher can by violence break into the intimate space of the hearer's intuitive data bank or tape storage room, and force-record faith over the older tapes of fear and disbelief found there.

It is here that the place of sin in this whole scheme or process requires treatment. There are, of course, tendencies to accept or reject the gospel, which may be traceable to trauma in early childhood or to bitter experience in churches even in adult life. There is a bottom line, however, where the hearer has to accept accountability for the choices made within the options open at the time. Ezekiel's fresh insight delivered to the exiles in Babylon still holds: One cannot blame parents or anyone else. The soul of the father *and* the soul of the son belong to God. And whichever of them makes the sinful choice, *that's* the one who will die for it (Ezek. 18:4). Parents are responsible for what they do with and to and for their children, but they only plant. The response to all influences is ultimately chargeable to the responder. Yes, Virginia, there is such a thing as sin, the willful refusal to seek, hear, and do the will of God, regardless of the charisma of those who present it. No generation can bear responsibility for what any other sinfully chooses, but it must carry its own load. And for the preacher, that includes responsibility for acquiring all the skill possible with which to proclaim the gospel. After that, as God told Ezekiel, the matter of whether people hear or not is up to them (Ezek. 3:11).

In summary, the vicarious experience of the gospel, here referred to as designed to be recorded on intuitive tapes, is offered by the preacher, to those who have ears to hear and hearts to heed. Positive responses on the part of the hearers are so essential that there can be no real preaching without them. Thus preacher and hearer are engaged in a kind of dialogue, whether audible or inaudible, and nowhere is the Protestant doctrine of the priesthood of all believers more apparent.

Now a final theological question underlies and flows out of all this discussion: What sort of innate nature is assumed to be in these persons to whom the gospel is preached? It has been hinted at as a tiny spark of the image of God already, but the question requires more detailed treatment. How far does one have to depart from orthodoxy to engage in the design of these experiential encounters with the gospel truth? Biblical answers range all the way from Paul's confessional implications of total depravity (Rom. 7:12-14) to the Genesis declarations that God made humans in the divine image (1:26) and that everything God made is good (1:31). M. Scott Peck, a current combiner of psychiatry and religion and author of the best-selling *People of the Lie,* has reluctantly confirmed the existence of at least some rare humans who are so evil as to strike a kind of terror in the heart of the therapist (pp. 64-65). Good-hearted veteran pastors everywhere have encountered at least one or two persons whose demonic tendencies force the pastor, regardless of theological training and tradition, to maintain some sort of doctrine of sin, even original sin. The suspicion, then, that this experiential approach is based on naive optimism about human nature would be ill-founded.

As I have stated, however, a hard and fast predestinarian view would leave no room for a preacher or healer of any kind to be meaningfully engaged in the gospel. Jesus implies by his word to the penitent thief on the cross that no healer has the right to give up on anybody who is still breathing. This would hold even though there might be good reason for a pastor-healer to refer a given person or patient to someone else. There is always *some* potential for hearing in every soul to whom the gospel is sent, and that includes the whole world. The estimates of the "wheat and tares" in any given group will vary, but there has to be an assumption on the part of the preacher that there are in every audience those for whom "it doth not yet appear what [they] shall be" (I John 3:2), in terms of spiritual growth. A preacher following this experience-centered approach must labor endlessly in the hope that what looks like a tare is actually wheat. That preacher, however, must be prepared to bear the sight of the opposite, or maximum appearance of defeat. In both cases, whether one is accustomed to reaching many and casting out the demonic, or not, the matter is finally in higher hands. Thus the methodology proposed here is compatible with all traditional doctrines of man save the extreme opposites of humanism and total depravity.

There is elaborated here a preaching methodology which proposes to remove only the first veil of mystery concerning how the Word acts to save, heal, and empower people. It explains how, to some degree, trust or belief may come from the Holy Spirit's use of the vicarious experience. This uncovering or demythologizing of the first or surface phase of the once-almost-magic impact of the Word, however, only renders the next phases of human response all the more awesome and clothed in mystery. It will always be a miracle of grace that despite the limitations of our best efforts, people are saved and healed and made whole. So it is still altogether appropriate, as one ponders the process, to exclaim with a preacher named Paul (Rom. 11:33): "O the depth of the riches both of the wisdom and knowledge of God! how unsearchable are his judgments, and his ways past finding out!"

SELECTED BIBLIOGRAPHY

Achtemeier, Elizabeth. *Creative Preaching*. Nashville: Abingdon, 1980.

Berne, Eric. *Intuition and Ego States*. New York: Harper & Row, 1977.
Brown, David M. *Dramatic Narrative in Preaching*. Valley Forge, Pa.: Judson Press, 1981.
Buttrick, David G. *Homiletic: Moves and Structures*. Philadelphia: Fortress Press, 1987.
Buttrick, George A. *The Parables of Jesus*. Garden City, N.Y.: Doubleday, Doran, 1928.

Cox, James W. *Preaching*. San Francisco: Harper & Row, 1985.
Craddock, Fred B. *As One Without Authority*. Nashville/New York: Abingdon Press, 1971.
———. *Overhearing the Gospel*. Nashville: Abingdon, 1978.
———. *Preaching*. Nashville: Abingdon Press, 1985.

Davis, H. Grady. *Design for Preaching*. Philadelphia: Fortress Press, 1958.

Eslinger, Richard L. *A New Hearing*. Nashville: Abingdon Press, 1987.

Fant, Clyde E. *Preaching for Today*. San Francisco: Harper & Row, 1987.
Forbes, James A., Jr. *The Holy Spirit and Preaching*. Nashville: Abingdon Press, 1989.

Jensen, R. A. *Telling the Story*. Minneapolis: Augsburg, 1980.

Leonard, George B. *Education and Ecstasy*. New York: Delacorte Press, 1968.
Lowry, Eugene L. *Doing Time in the Pulpit*. Nashville: Abingdon Press, 1985.
———. *How to Preach a Parable*. Nashville: Abingdon Press, 1989.

Markquart, Edward F. *Quest for Better Preaching*. Minneapolis: Augsburg, 1985.

Massey, James E. *Designing the Sermon*. Nashville: Abingdon, 1980.

Mitchell, Henry H. *Black Preaching*. San Francisco: Harper & Row, 1979.

Mitchell, Henry H., and Nicholas C. Lewter. *Soul Theology*. San Francisco: Harper & Row, 1986.

Pannenberg, Wolfhart. "Focal Essay: The Revelation of God in Jesus of Nazareth," in *Theology as History*, James M. Robinson and John B. Cobb, eds. New York: Harper & Row, 1967.

———. "Faith and Reason," in *Basic Questions in Theology*, vol. 2. Philadelphia: Fortress Press, 1971.

———. *The Apostles' Creed in the Light of Today's Questions*. Philadelphia: Westminster Press, 1972.

Peck, M. Scott. *People of the Lie*. New York: Simon & Schuster, 1983.

Ricoeur, Paul. "Paul Ricoeur on Biblical Hermeneutics," in *Semeia 4*, ed. John Dominic Crossan. Society of Biblical Literature, 1975.

TeSelle, Sallie McFague. *Speaking in Parables*. Philadelphia: Fortress Press, 1975.

Watson, J. V. "Two Sermons by Brother Carper: The Eloquent Negro Preacher," in *Tales and Takings, Sketches and Incidents, from the Itinerant and Editorial Budget of Rev. J. V. Watson, Editor of the Northwestern Christian Advocate*. New York, 1856. Quoted by Russell Ritchie, and H. Dean Trulear, in *American Baptist Quarterly*, vol. 71, no. 1, March 1987.

I N D E X